PERCEPTIONS

HEALING FROM DISTORTIONS OF GOD, SELF, & OTHERS

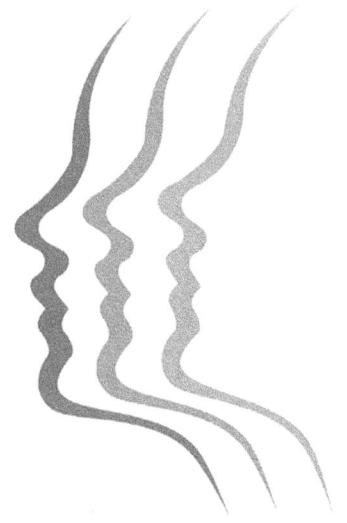

LYNN ELDRIDGE
WITH DR. RANDY CLARK

Copyright © 2024 by Lynn Eldridge

All rights reserved. No part of this publication may be reproduced, distributed, or transmitted in any form or by any means, including photocopying, recording, or other electronic or mechanical methods, without the prior written permission of the publisher, except in the case of brief quotations embodied in critical reviews and certain other noncommercial uses permitted by copyright law.

For permission requests, email contact@lynneldridge.com

www.lynneldridge.com

Cover Design: Briton Media

Editing and Page Design: Ashley Hagan @Inkwellwriters.com

Paperback ISBN: 978-1-7374906-4-7

eBook ISBN: 978-1-7374906-5-4

Scripture quotations marked AMPC are taken from the Amplified Bible Copyright 1954, 1958, 1962, 1964,1965, 1987, 2015 (only use the last year corresponding to the edition quoted) by The Lockman Foundation.

All Scripture marked with the designation "GW" is taken from GOD'S WORD®.
© 1995, 2003, 2013, 2014, 2019, 2020 by God's Word to the Nations Mission Society.
Used by permission.

Scripture quotations marked MSG are taken from The Message, copyright © 1993, 2002, 2018 by Eugene H. Peterson. Used by permission of NavPress. All rights reserved. Represented by Tyndale House Publishers.

Scripture quotations marked (NKJV) are taken from the New King James Version®. Copyright © 1982 by Thomas Nelson. Used by permission. All rights reserved.

Scripture quotations marked (NLT) are taken from the Holy Bible, New Living Translation, copyright ©1996, 2004, 2015 by Tyndale House Foundation. Used by permission of Tyndale House Publishers, Carol Stream, Illinois 60188. All rights reserved.

Scripture quotations marked NIV are taken from the Holy Bible, New International Version®, NIV®. Copyright © 1973, 1978, 1984, 2011 by Biblica, Inc.™ Used by permission of Zondervan. All rights reserved worldwide. www.zondervan.com. The "NIV" and "New International Version" are trademarks registered in the United States Patent and Trademark Office by Biblica, Inc.™

Scripture quotations marked TPT are from The Passion Translation®. Copyright © 2017, 2018, 2020 by Passion & Fire Ministries, Inc. Used by permission. All rights reserved. ThePassionTranslation.com.

PRAISE FOR *PERCEPTIONS*

Like many who spent the majority of their adult life in pastoral ministry, I logged in countless hours in counseling, working people through the damage that life's events had in their life. Somewhere along the way, I discovered that sometimes one's perceived reality may not be one's actual reality. Because of blind spots and filters, sometimes it is one's interpretation of life's events and environments that create their perception. That means that you are not shaped by your environment as much as you are by your perception of your environment. I remember a few times when my siblings and I would gather and talk about our growing up years together, and afterwards I would walk away wondering if we even grew up in the same house together. Their memory of some childhood events and mine were not the same. Lynn Eldridge in her book, *Perceptions: Healing from Distortions of God, Self, and Others,* illustrates the truth through sharing her own past and what shaped or skewed her perception of reality. The book not only sheds light on common blind spots but also on processes to discover them and get through them. I appreciate Lynn's vulnerability to share her own struggles and the processes she worked through as she pursued her own freedom. For many, it will give some clarity to their own struggles and solutions of actions to take that really work. The reflection and action steps at the end of the chapters helps make this book very practical. For those who more easily learn through the practical illustrations of another's life, you are going to love this book. I certainly recommend it.

Dr. Rodney Hogue, Founder of Rodney Hogue Ministries, speaker, and author of *Forgiveness*

The life and ministry of Lynn of Eldridge is a beautiful expression of God's heart to this world. Her authenticity of heart is beyond compelling, and her love for God and people is both deep and enduring. Lynn is one of my heroes in the "faith." I am honored to endorse such an amazing daughter of God, and I celebrate her life-giving words in this book.

Larry Randolph, Pastor of Peytonsville Baptist Church in Thompson's Station, Tennessee, and President of Living Rain Ministries

Lynn is a woman of true faith in Jesus and embodies a life of pure restoration. *Perceptions* explains how what we see and what we believe shape everything we are. If we get our perception right, everything else will flow from that place and fall into line. Lynn never gives up on people because she believes exactly what she teaches in her book. I have seen her live this out first hand. Read this book with the Lord and allow Him to heal places in your heart you didn't know needed healing, to set you free, and to give you the correct perception of your life so you can live in the freedom Jesus paid for you to live in.

Will Hart, Founder of Will Hart Ministries, CEO of Iris Global, author of *Godrunner*

Lynn Eldridge's newest book, *Perceptions: Healing from Distortions of God, Self, and Others,* is a transparent journey into the revelation of what brings brokenness and wounds to the soul, affecting every area of life. Along with Dr. Randy Clark, Lynn shares with us truths that she has learned from the Holy Spirit of emotional healing, freedom, and complete peace found in living with Jesus. This is a powerful addition to your spiritual and mental health resources that I highly recommend.

Dr. Mike Hutchings, President, God Heals PTSD Foundation, Global Awakening Ministry Associate and author of *Supernatural Healing From the Captivity of Trauma*

Lynn Eldridge's book, *Perceptions: Healing from the Distortions of God, Self, and Others,* is a powerful, Spirit-filled journey into the hidden places of the heart where many of us wrestle with distorted perceptions. Lynn brings clarity to how our past wounds and judgments can cloud our understanding of God and hinder our relationships with others. This book is a treasure for anyone looking to break free from the lies that have held them back and step into the fullness of God's love and truth. Lynn's honest storytelling and practical guidance will help you see yourself and your Creator through the lens of healing and grace.

Tyler Feller, Founder of Encounter Night, and author of *Don't Stop*

"We awaken in others the same attitude of mind we hold toward them."
— ELBERT HUBBARD

"It's not what you look at that matters; it's what you see."
— HENRY DAVID THOREAU

TABLE OF CONTENTS

INTRODUCTION

1: INNER HEALING IS LIFE-CHANGING   1

2: DISTORTION & DYSFUNCTION   13

3: BITTER ROOT JUDGMENTS & EXPECTATIONS   23

4: HOW JUDGMENTS AFFECT YOU   31

5: ATTITUDES ARE INDICATORS   47

6: RESPOND OR REACT?   57

7: FOOD FOR THOUGHT   67

8: LOVE IS THE ANSWER   75

ACKNOWLEDGEMENTS   83

ABOUT THE AUTHORS   85

APPENDIX   91

INTRODUCTION

Why is it that two people can look at the same thing but see it differently? Why do some people see the glass as half-full and others see it as half-empty? I spent decades living with a false perception of myself and others, but now I am grateful for an undistorted understanding that brings clarity, fulfillment, satisfaction, and love. It began with a painful awareness that my "best" thinking didn't work and that I needed to put down the "freedom" of doing what felt good when I wanted, how I wanted, and with whom I wanted. This way of thinking had only ever brought me pain, torment, and depression. I had to discover the real freedom that I had all I've ever wanted all along, but I just couldn't perceive it. I went from suicidal idealizations to great joy and a passion to live life to the fullest. I was blind but now I see.

There were many reasons why my perceptions of myself, other people, and even God, were so distorted. I felt, saw, and heard my own inner pain, fear, and torment, and I couldn't enjoy or appreciate the gifts that I did have. I wasn't grateful for anything. I eventually got to the point of suicide. I had tried "everything." I had lived in multiple states and many countries. I went to the "best" doctors, sought out the "best" religions – always looking but never finding. I was grasping at the wind. Pain and more pain was all I saw, all I knew, and all I expected.

According to the world's standards, I had a "good life" – a beautiful, paid-off home, exotic cars, luxurious clothing and jewels. I lacked for nothing outside of me, but the way I saw everything was through the lens of lack. I craved happiness. I didn't know the ways of the One who changed everything. I kind of knew Jesus Christ, but my perception of Him was that He was angry, punishing, and disappointed, and I felt I could never be perfect enough for Him. That false perception of God stemmed from my perception of my mother as a child. I judged her even as a little girl. I saw her as angry, punishing, and disappointed in me. Then I saw God as angry, punishing, and disappointed in me. I perceived everything through the mirror of my own heart which was full of rejection, unforgiveness, judgments, trauma, and pain. I was angry, punishing, and disappointed in myself. It distorted my perception of everything.

Today I know that I am loved by the One who is the God of Love. His name is Jesus. He's not angry. He's not disappointed in me. He is for me – not against me. He has good plans for me, to give me hope and a future. I am made in His image, and He is beautiful. He is Beauty itself.

We are the BELOVED'S. It is a love story.

Learning God's ways – like seeking Him in prayer, reading His Word, forgiveness, and the principle of sowing and reaping – alters our perception and outlook in all of our relationships. As my perceptions of Him and His ways changed, it has brought me hope, healing, and freedom from the disorders that had plagued me. I learned I was loved, and I responded to that love. The One I thought I hated became the One who showed me mercy, kindness, and compassion. He truly restored my soul. I understand now. I "see" now. His ways are not rules to follow but tools of life and love. I thought I hated Him, but I hated religion because religion wants to punish. I also hated myself. Now, through the corrective lens of love, I have learned He's a good Father and His ways are protective.

Just as the universe is held together by the principles of physics in operation, there are also Godly principles continuously in action. The orbits of the planets, the rising of the sun, the going and coming of the tides, and the changing of seasons – all of these things continue in motion whether we want them to or not. We can't break them, and if we try to, they could break us. It doesn't matter whether or not we believe in these physical principles; they apply to us regardless of how true we think they are. We can't pretend gravity doesn't exist and not be affected by it anymore.

It's the same with Godly principles. God created laws for us to live by, not to control us or make us miserable but for our protection and our good. If we go against them because we don't like them, it could break us, just like with the physical laws of the universe. Abraham Lincoln said, "My concern is not whether God is on my side; my greatest concern is to be on God's side, for God is always right." Going against God's principles could feel right for a time, but in the end, the consequences are real and sometimes devastating. It leads to error and pain.

When we were children, we may not have understood why our mother would be so "mean" to us when we wanted to cross the street without her. We didn't know what we didn't know. Maybe there was a car coming, but because we had no understanding of the consequences, we didn't understand why *she* would cause us this pain. As we developed some life skills, we understood why. We didn't even see the car coming, nor did we understand why, in our *perception*, she was angry and mean.

Of course, now we do! It's the same with God and His principles. They are designed for our safety, not to take away our freedom.

King David said, "Give me understanding, so that I may keep your law and obey it with all my heart" (Psalm 119:34, NIV). According to a commentary I read, David was around seventeen years old when he wrote that psalm. He knew and perceived that God was good even when he didn't have the understanding or maturity to see where his problems and issues were coming from. But as He continued to pursue God – even when He didn't understand – He knew that the answer was always God.

I share my own story in this book to prove how easy it is to allow unforgiveness and past wounds to distort our view of our Creator and those He created. When we view ourselves and others through a lens of pain, our response is to be defensive, unforgiving, critical, and offended. And in return, we cause those same responses in others. When we allow the Lord to heal us from the inside out, it frees us. Our perceptions mirror our childhood environment and our experiences, and also Satan tries to twist things in order to steal, kill, and destroy. The curse of bitter root judgments and expectations can cause us to view present circumstances through the distorted lens of past wounds. We find ourselves reacting to people or situations because they remind us of what we have experienced before, even when the new situation has nothing to do with that old wound. Our response is like pressing a wound that we didn't realize was there. Part of maturing in Christ includes recognizing childish or selfish behavior and noticing that when we react in a childish way, it is probably because it is triggering an emotional response from a childhood wound. When we recognize that wound and forgive the person for the hurt, we are healed from it and can move forward in maturity. And ultimately, love is the answer to walking in forgiveness and freedom in our relationships. The more we grow in love for God, ourselves, and others, the more peace, joy, and hope we have in life.

Years ago, when I came back into the church, I was so hungry for more of God. One day, I was driving home, thanking God for setting me free of bipolar, suicide, addiction, and all the rest. I asked Him, "Is this all there is? Going to church on Sundays and being a 'good girl?' I find it hard to believe that the One who puts the stars in the sky and knows them by name is boring. Isn't there more?" My phone rang. It was a friend of mine telling me that a group of people were going to a conference in Des Moines, Iowa, to see a guy named Randy Clark. I had never heard of Randy Clark. All I knew was that my friend was a trusted source. If he was going, I was going! I immediately booked a flight. Dr. Randy Clark is a pastor, speaker, and author of many books, and is probably best known as the evangelist who was an integral part of the Toronto outpouring in 1994. What I didn't know yet is that he had written a book called There's More. *The conference that I attended was in 2012. I was amazingly touched by the power and love of God at that conference, and I will never be the same! I found out there is more to my relationship with God, and it's anything but boring!*

I honor and respect the balance of the Word and power of God through the leadership of Dr. Clark in his organization, Global Awakening. I am at a loss for words to express my gratitude for all that Dr. Clark has done to help me and countless others encounter the love and power of God in a Biblically-based way. I was delighted when he agreed to include a chapter for this book about a subject that goes hand in hand with the concept of how our perceptions shape our interactions with God and one another.

1

INNER HEALING IS LIFE-CHANGING
By Dr. Randy Clark

> *"Have mercy on me, O God, according to Your unfailing love. According to Your great compassion, blot out my iniquity and cleanse me from my sin. Behold, I was brought forth in iniquity, and in sin my mother conceived me. Behold, You desire truth in the inward parts, and in the hidden part You will make me to know wisdom."*
> Psalm 51:1-6 (NIV)

As a pastor for over thirty years, I've found that sometimes, no matter what you tell people or how much you try to help them, people don't seem to change. For a long time, I wondered why. I've now discovered that in many cases, people need inner healing in order to have lasting change in their lives. We need the experience of God healing our past hurts, offenses, and traumas in order to produce lasting change.

People say that what we believe affects how we feel, and there's some truth to that. But sometimes what we feel blocks what we believe from going from our head to our emotions. It blocks us from having an emotional experience with God, and it clouds our view of reality.

For example, I had a man named Dr. Victor Matthews come speak to our church in the mid-1990s. When I met him, Dr. Matthews was seventy years old. He had a ThD (Doctor of Theology) and had been teaching religion, theology, and Biblical studies for fifty years. Dr. Matthews was full of joy, and he loved helping people enter into the joy of the presence of God, but it had only been the last two years of his life that he truly experienced that joy himself. He explained that in the past he could teach about God's grace and mercy and see people experience it for themselves, but he had personally never experienced it. He felt locked up emotionally. He said, "I knew in my head the truth, but I'd never experienced it in my emotions." It was like he had a wall around his heart.

When he was sixty-eight years old, Dr. Matthews attended an inner healing session at the Evanston Vineyard Church, and during that experience, he asked the Lord to show him where the wall around his heart began. The Lord showed him a vision of himself at three years old. In the vision, he remembered an incident in which he had come inside the house crying about something that had happened to him. His father was of Scandinavian descent, and instead of comforting him, he slapped him across the face and said, "Victor, we Matthews do not cry. So, get ahold of yourself."

As an adult, Dr. Matthews understood that his father had been raised in a family that didn't show emotion. While he was a good man, a moral man, a man who provided for his family, when it came to affection, he was an iceberg. "This event of being slapped as a little boy and told to stop crying was where I began to build a wall around my heart," Dr. Matthews explained, "because when I needed my daddy, he wasn't there emotionally for me." The wall was built to protect himself against the risk of rejection, and that wall continued into adulthood.

During the inner healing session at the Evanston Vineyard Church, Dr. Matthews realized he couldn't take the wall down himself. He said to the Lord, "You're either going to have to come over it or come around it, but I can't take it down." It was all he had known, and he felt powerless to tear it down. But in the experience of this vision, in prayer, that's exactly what the Lord did. He came around and took that little boy – not the sixty-eight-year-old Dr. Victor Matthews, but the three-year-old little boy – and hugged him. He wept, and then he rejoiced. He entered into the joy of the Lord. Then he taught others about his experience because he didn't want people to go through what he had for most of his life.

Theology alone wasn't able to break down the wall. Dr. Matthews had a ThD. He taught theology. Sometimes we can believe the right things, but we have to allow the Lord to experientially heal us on the inside by the Holy Spirit in order to unlock our hearts.

Inner healing can happen in a counseling session, it can happen when God sovereignly reveals something to us, and sometimes it can happen through prophecy. I believe that a lot of prophetic ministry has an inner healing aspect to it. Words of knowledge often deal with healing of the physical body, but prophetic ministry often brings healing to the soul. It deals with how we perceive ourselves, how we perceive others, and how we perceive God. Revelation comes from a prophetic word. That's why I think Paul had such a value on prophecy, because he saw the power prophecy had to express the love of God. To build up. To comfort. To encourage. The inner healing ministry has those same dynamics.

In my own life, my issue was that I was extremely insecure. It was difficult for me to believe that God would come through for me. I believed if someone else said, "Come, Holy Spirit," that He would come. But if *I* said, "Come, Holy Spirit," He *might* come. Some of that stemmed from growing up with my dad. Just like Dr. Matthews, my father was also a good man. He worked eighty hours a week in the oil fields for most of his life and farmed on the side. He worked hard to provide for us, and that's how he showed his love. It was only when my dad was experiencing the power of the Holy Spirit that he expressed affection for us. That was the only time he was able to tell us that he loved us.

I was involved in a lot of sports, and I remember in high school looking up into the bleachers to see if my dad was able to make the games. It wasn't that he didn't want to come; he often worked double shifts in the oil fields as a driller. I never questioned his love for me, or his provision, or his acceptance. What I doubted was whether I could depend on him to show up. So when I went to minister, that same feeling of doubt was with me.

In the 1990s, right before I left to minister at the Airport Vineyard Church in Toronto, people would ask me, "What do you think's going to happen when you go to Toronto?" and I would say, "Well, I *hope* God shows up." Even my twelve-year-old son told me I didn't have any faith. The night before I left for Toronto, a businessman friend of mine gave me a prophetic word. He said, "Test me now, test me now, test me now. Do not be afraid. I will back you up. I want your eyes to be opened to see my resources for you in the heavenlies, as Elisha prayed that Gehazi's eyes would be opened. And do not become anxious, because when you become anxious, you can't hear me." That word literally healed the fear that God wouldn't show up for me. Sometimes inner healing can happen when you receive the right word at the right time. *"A word fitly spoken is like apples of gold in settings of silver"* (Proverbs 25:11). It can set people free.

In Toronto, I was scheduled to teach at the Airport Vineyard Church for four days, and it turned into a full-fledged revival that lasted twelve and a half years! Yet, in the early days of the revival, I still needed inner healing, so God began working on me during the day even while I was being used powerfully in the night services.

One day I was driving somewhere with Carol Arnott and a man named Steve, when Carol started asking me questions. I don't know if she could sense my insecurity or if the Lord gave her prophetic insight. She said to me, "You did well in school, didn't you?"

I said, "Yes, I did. Honor rolls. Dean's list."

"Did you feel driven to do well?"

"Yeah, I wanted to do well."

"Do you care what people think about you? Do you fish for compliments?"

I said, "Yes, too much. That's a hook of mine. I really want to be accepted. I want attention. I need to hear someone say, 'You did well.'"

"Why do you think you're that way?"

Well, I had that figured out. My dad only had an eighth-grade education. His mother was illiterate. I was the first boy to make it beyond eighth grade in our family line. My father wanted us to do well in school, so he offered us a dollar for every A. Now a dollar back in the late fifties was worth a lot more than it is today! He offered a dollar for every A, nothing for B's, and if I got less than a B, I had to pay him back a dollar. I got ten dollars for being on the Honor Roll. So I told Carol that's why I wanted to succeed.

She said, "I don't think it has anything to do with that."

This about blew me away. I thought I had figured out why I had a performance mentality; it was because I had been programmed as a boy. I challenged her.

"I think it has everything to do with it."

She said, "I don't think so." Then she said, "You were conceived out of wedlock, weren't you?"

I said that I was, but that didn't have anything to do with me. It was my mom and dad's sin, and they had repented and gotten married. That was their stuff. Then she told me she wanted me to watch a video about inner healing.

I was convinced she was wrong and I was right. Until I watched the video. By the end of the video, I was so convinced by the evidence of the scientific research it presented, I was in tears. At the end of the video, I believed she was right and I was wrong. So I began the process of inner healing during the day, and I would pull myself together enough to allow God to move through me at night.

The video on inner healing challenged my worldview. Up until that point, my worldview had been that we are born with a clean slate, and then we grow up and sin. I believed everything had to do with our own will. What inner healing taught me is that we aren't born with a clean slate. David got it right in Psalm 51, which is an Old Testament window into a New Testament understanding of grace. According to the law, David had no business asking for what he was asking for, which was mercy. He had committed intentional sin. It wasn't just a weakness. He planned it out, he strategized it. But in this psalm, we have the greatest insight in the Bible into the issue of sin and the nature of grace. It's as powerful and strong as anything in the New Testament.

"Have mercy on me, O God, according to your unfailing love. According to your great compassion, blot out my iniquity and cleanse me from my sin. Behold, I was brought forth in iniquity, and in sin my mother conceived me. Behold, You desire truth in the inward parts, and in the hidden part You will make me to know wisdom" (Psalm 51:1-6).

I never really believed that part about being brought forth in iniquity and conceived in sin. I knew it was in the Bible, but I didn't believe it meant what it said. Because of my worldview, I thought it couldn't actually mean we had sin right from the start. It had to mean something else. This inner healing experience changed my perception. We aren't born with a clean slate. Sin is already there. There are tendencies already there through our family line, even in the womb.

There are three words that are translated to mean sin in the Bible: transgression, iniquity, and sin. In Hebrew, *transgression* means you've betrayed someone's trust. *Sin* means that you are walking along a slippery path, and even though you are trying not to fall, you slip. It doesn't have to be intentional. Sin is not necessarily something you planned or willed to do. You could have been trying your hardest but still slipped and fell. The word *iniquity* means that from birth you were born with a sin nature that is twisted; you inherited it from your parents. You actually aren't born with a clean slate.

I found out my will was not nearly as free as I thought. There are some sins in our family lines that we have a strong predisposition toward. It's hereditary in the same way that we share our family's DNA. Because I didn't believe that, my understanding of sin was that it was entirely a matter of my own will. If there was something in my life that I couldn't seem to get free from, then it had to be me. I didn't have enough willpower. I was weak. It was all my fault. And if you believe that you started with a clean slate and that all the stuff you've got going wrong in your life is your fault because you made wrong decisions, you can become very critical of yourself. You can feel hopeless, and I was.

Looking back over my life, I could see certain areas of strong temptation. Sexual temptation was so strong for me when I was a young minister, I built protections around myself – like to never be alone with a member of the opposite sex. During inner healing sessions, the Lord began to remind me of my family's history. My mother was born two months after her parents got married. My father was born seven months after his parents got married. My grandfather was a womanizer before he got saved. I began to understand that it's not just genes that we inherit from our parents. That sexual temptation had been passed down to me.

One of the questions Carol asked me that had a huge impact was whether it was easy for me to receive affection from my mother. It wasn't. As a matter of fact, while I didn't understand why, I had always, even as a child, resisted her hugs and kisses. She never abused me in any way. I had no reason to run from her affection, but whenever she would try to hug or kiss me, I would back away. What I began to understand is that when she was pregnant with me – out of wedlock in a small town where everybody knew everybody else's business – she carried me in shame. She didn't want to be pregnant in that way. What she passed down to me was a message of rejection. Rejection causes you to need to prove you have a right to exist in the world. You fish for compliments. You say, "Notice me!" You want to succeed. You're driven, and you don't even understand why. I thought it was my dad's dollars that were driving me to succeed, but it was something more powerful than his money. It was a deep, psychological, spiritual issue. When I was starving for affection and couldn't get it from my mother because of some deep, psychological issue that I didn't even realize I had, I turned to other things or other people to fill that need.

When I began to understand the underlying causes of my temptation, all of a sudden I was more merciful to myself. I realized my will was not as free as I thought it was. There were some really huge things going on in my subconscious that I didn't even have any understanding of, and they were setting me up for certain types of behavior. Now I found it easier to forgive myself, and I also understood that I couldn't fix it myself. God had to do it. No education in the world would fix it.

Carol suggested that I forgive my mom, which surprised me. My mother hadn't done anything wrong. But when I forgave my mom for carrying me when she didn't want me, it freed me. The next time I saw my mom, I kissed her. It was the first time I had ever kissed her, and I was forty-two years old at the time. Now I am able to show her affection every time I see her, and I also encouraged her to forgive her own mother who was pregnant with her out of wedlock.

Going back to Psalm 51, David says, *"Surely You desire truth in the inner parts, and You teach me wisdom in the inmost place. Cleanse me with hyssop and I will be clean. Wash me and I'll be whiter than snow. Let me hear joy and gladness. Let the bones that You've crushed, rejoice. Hide Your face from my sins and blot out my iniquity. Create in me a clean heart, O God, and renew a steadfast spirit within me. Do not cast me from Your presence, or take Your Holy Spirit from me. Restore to me the joy of Your salvation and grant a willing spirit to sustain me. Then I will teach transgressors Your ways and sinners will turn back to You. Save me from blood guilt, O God, the God who saves me. And my tongue will sing of Your righteousness. Oh, Lord, open my lips and my mouth will declare Your praise. You do not delight in sacrifice or I would bring it. You do not take pleasure in burnt offerings. The sacrifices of God are a broken spirit. A broken and a contrite heart, O God, these You will not despise"* (Psalm 51:10-17).

And yet, God also says He will bind up the brokenhearted (Psalm 147:3). What does it mean to have a broken spirit? I believe it means to be vulnerable, to recognize that you need a touch from God. David understood that it was not religious sacrifices that would heal him but honesty and vulnerability in the presence of God. It's realizing that we are broken and that only God can put us back together. *"A broken and contrite heart, O God, you will not despise."*

Inner healing is going through the process of sanctification and becoming who God says we are. We are free, and we are forgiven. He wants us to not only be free in our understanding, but we should be experientially free as well. He wants us to experience His righteousness. When it comes to our relationship with God, we understand that justice is getting what you deserve, mercy is not getting what you deserve, and grace is getting what you don't deserve – in a positive sense. But grace is more than undeserved forgiveness. It's more than getting gifts that we don't deserve. One of the meanings of grace is a divine enablement. We need to believe that God is willing to give divine enablement beyond our human capacity or we are just behaviorists. We are just changing our behavior. Grace comes from beyond us and helps us do what we couldn't do in our own strength or capacity. Grace not only forgives the sin, it gives us the power to live differently. But with grace, there needs to come truth. Until we get some understanding of truth, it's hard for grace to bring about the full work that God wants it to in our life because we're actually believing the lie of the enemy rather than the truth of God. That is where theology is important.

The other lesson I received in Toronto was that the things I needed healing from were affecting more than just me; they were affecting the way I was raising my family. For example, at that time, my children had never spent the night at my parents' house. I had a twelve-year-old son, an eight-year-old daughter, a three-year-old son, and a one-year-old son, and none of them had ever spent the night at their grandparents' house. They had spent the night with my wife's parents, but not with mine. Carol reminded me that inner healing wasn't a one-time thing. I needed to open myself up for the Holy

Spirit to bring to mind any areas where I needed to forgive my parents so I could deal with them.

The Lord brought to my remembrance a time when I was about five years old. Now, as an adult, I can look back on my parents with sympathy and understand that my dad was working eighty hours a week and my mother had three children by the time she was twenty-three. Quite honestly, I'm surprised my mother did as well as she did with what she had to overcome. But as a little boy, I didn't have that understanding. One day I was outside riding my tricycle while she was hanging out the laundry. I don't remember what happened, but she walked over, pointed her finger at me, and said, "When you grow up and have kids, don't bring them over here with their dirty diapers and expect me to change them.

And as a little boy of five, I remember looking up at her and saying, "Don't worry. I never will."

That was a vow that I had forgotten I had even made. I was not aware of the subconscious drive that was causing me to make an irrational decision like refusing to allow my kids to spend the night with their grandparents. I had to forgive my mother and break that vow.

With forgiveness, I didn't have to bring each and every thing to my mother. It wouldn't have been helpful to bring up every way I hurt her or she hurt me! It was the spiritual principle of forgiving her and breaking vows that caused a change in me. It was getting rid of those bitter root judgments. Inner healing allows us to grow up in Jesus and to become more and more free. What else is sanctification than getting more and more free? And it should be experiential. It's applying the truth of God's word and making yourself available to the grace of the Spirit. We need to change our spiritual heritage, and we can. In my family, my oldest son was born six years after my wife and I were married, and all of my children have had very Godly experiences in meeting and marrying their spouses. That generational sexual sin that had been passed down in my family line is broken!

We can call those things generational curses, but I don't think that's the best word for it. It's something that was passed down spiritually, in the same way that we inherit the color of our eyes or the way we speak. It's the things that we wish we weren't, or the things we wish we didn't feel. We are not a blank slate. And I want you to know that while some things can be healed with inner healing, sometimes there are situations that are actually stemming from a demonic source, either through your family line, something that was done to you, or something you gave yourself to. In those situations, you feel captive, but Jesus came to set the captives free. I think to say we don't need inner healing, or to believe that as a Christian we are never bothered by the demonic, is not as helpful as it may sound. If in reality you are fighting these battles and losing, and then repenting but losing again in an endless cycle, it can feel pretty hopeless. It can leave you wondering why you can't get victory. But if you understand that there's more than just your own will involved, and if you see that these sin issues stem from family patterns you had no control over, this is actually good news! Then you realize that it isn't your lack of willpower or your own weakness that causes you to struggle. In your own strength you may not be able to win the battle, but God's inner healing can set you free from those family strongholds. The truth of God's Word with the grace of His Spirit can bring lasting healing, not only in you, but in your whole family line.

Dr. Randy Clark

2

DISTORTION & DYSFUNCTION

The eye is the lamp of the body; so if your eye is clear [spiritually perceptive], your whole body will be full of light [benefiting from God's precepts]. But if your eye is bad [spiritually blind], your whole body will be full of darkness [devoid of God's precepts]. So if the [very] light inside you [your inner self, your heart, your conscience] is darkness, how great and terrible is that darkness!"
Matthew 6:22-23 (AMPC)

Our attitudes and perceptions are mirrors of our heart, and they typically reflect two things: our experiences and our childhood environment. We are imprinted by the attitudes and perceptions of our parents or other authority figures from our childhood years. It's like the phrase, "Monkey see, monkey do." Children are incredibly impressionable, and they pick up their parents' perceptions of life, themselves, and others. We grow up thinking and seeing through our family's lens of life, and we adopt that perception as our own, even if it is distorted.

I read an article once that said scientists had looked into a black hole in space. Instead of being just nothingness and darkness, everything in it was distorted, like a funhouse mirror at a circus. That's what the enemy does with our perceptions. The definition of *distortion* is "to cause to be perceived unnaturally." It comes from the prefix *dis-* and the word *torque*. Dis was the Roman god of the underworld, and as a prefix, it means *the opposite*. Torque means *to twist*. So, to distort something is to *twist* it into the *opposite* of what it is. To distort is to create an optical illusion.

That Roman god of the underworld is just another name for Satan, the one who wants to steal, kill, and destroy. Satan wants us to believe the opposite – the distortion – of what is true. He wants us to believe the optical illusion. So if God wants us to live courageously, the enemy of our souls wants us to be DIScouraged. God gives us appointed times for things to happen, but the enemy wants us DISappointed because it doesn't happen in our timing. God wants us to honor and be honored. The enemy of our souls wants us to be DISHonored.

One of Satan's tactics is to distort our natural instincts. When I was a young girl and suffered from anorexia, I perceived myself as fat and ugly even when I weighed ninety pounds. I saw myself through that funhouse mirror, and I tried to control my pain with food. Satan twists our instinct for food into eating disorders. He twists our instinct for intimacy in the marriage bed into perversions. He twists our instinct for provision into greed. He twists the instinct to fill our hearts with God into idolatry as we seek things outside of Him to fill the voids. We chase after cheap thrills instead of hungering for the only One who satisfies.

My childhood environment was one of disappointment, criticism, and shame. It seemed that nothing I did was ever good enough. Real or imagined, I began to internalize the thought that I was not good enough. I was conceived out of wedlock, and my parents hastily married. This was not the life my mother had planned, and she projected that disappointment onto me. Because it's natural to take what your parents say as THE truth, I learned to adopt that disappointed perception that my mother had of me. It was the same perception that she received from her mother, who was an orphan who was horrifically abused emotionally and physically. They both did the best that they knew how, and our family perceived that as "normal."

Then, in grade school, a teacher criticized me in front of my peers. This experience also heavily shaped my perception of myself, which was that all women in authority saw me as I was: not good enough. Subconsciously, I lived my adult life having that attitude toward myself, and eventually I saw others as not good enough, either.

The problem is that anything negative that is sustained, like critical, hateful, or bitter attitudes, can distort our perceptions of reality. What we see through the distorted lens of pain and negativity becomes our reality, whether it is real or imagined. That deceptive perception leads us to make choices or decisions that are inaccurate and bring us more instability, hurt, pain, and other consequences. Then we remain stuck thinking we are "victims of others," when in truth we are victims of our own attitudes and perceptions.

My distorted perception caused me to be hyper-critical of myself as well as towards other women. I would hear women talking and take it personally as if they were criticizing me. Then I'd react and reject them. This led to a never-ending cycle of allowing my attitudes to blind me to the truth – that there is nothing "wrong" with me or them. I was simply believing lies about myself that were formed from years of my perception-distorting experiences and environment.

Matthew 6:22-23 says, *"The eye is the lamp of the body; so if your eye is clear [spiritually perceptive], your whole body will be full of light [benefiting from God's precepts]. But if your eye is bad [spiritually blind], your whole body will be full of darkness [devoid of God's precepts]. So, if the [very] light inside you [your inner self, your heart, your conscience] is darkness, how great and terrible is that darkness!"*

Why was I so blind for so long? I did not know the ways I was created to function. My computer is a Mac. I cannot use PC instructions on my Mac. If I do, my computer won't function. It's not because my computer hates me. It's because it was not created to function that way, and it doesn't matter how I feel about it. The computer isn't punishing me. It's not angry with me. My computer doesn't care what I believe or what I think is best. It is not broken, mentally ill, or against me.

It was the same with me and my perception of God. I lived in dysfunction as long as I was ignorant of the ways I was created to function. I wanted to do what I wanted, when I wanted, how I wanted, and with whom I wanted. I was seeking "freedom," but I was walking into traps of bondage and reaping the consequences. When I was diagnosed as "mentally ill," it was actually the repercussions of unforgiveness, rebellion, self-will, self-centeredness, and selfishness on steroids! I was imploding within because my heart hated to be told what to do. My perception of authority figures was distorted because I had been abused by them in the past. God did not let this happen. People let this happen. It was not because God didn't care. It was because people, like me, didn't care.

So, if I want to live a good life, and perceive reality, I need to know the ways I was created to function. My Creator said to live in the ways of love and obedience IF I want to live a good life. Obedience is not being forced to do God's will; we do God's will because when we are touched by pure love, we want to know more about what love looks like. Love is life-building and healing – emotionally, mentally, physically, and relationally.

When there's a hurricane, there's peace and stillness in the middle – in the eye. Yet, there's debris stirred up all around it. We perceive God, ourselves, and others through the clarity or debris in our souls. The winds of life can stir up debris in the atmosphere. In my life, the debris was unforgiveness, judgments, negative thoughts, words, attitudes, emotions, motives, and behaviors. But I was "free" to do what I wanted to do. The lie of selfishness is that I wasn't hurting anyone but myself. The debris of the self-willed person creates more debris as it flies around. I believed I was only hurting myself, but in reality, that debris was flying around my life with hurricane force. It was wounding others and destroying everything and everyone around me.

Hurt people hurt people.
Healed people heal people.
And, of course, what we sow (or do), we will reap. How do we stop the madness that causes more madness and insanity?

TRAUMA: TO DISTORT YOUR IDENTITY AND STEAL YOUR DESTINY

While I was in a facility for mental health treatment, a counselor suggested that I write out the three most traumatic events in my life. Now, I was in treatment because I was out of control emotionally – in my thinking, in my behavior, and in my relationships – and I was escaping the discomfort of being with myself by any means I could find. I was uncomfortable in my own skin. I couldn't outrun myself, and when I had tried everything I thought would help me, and it didn't, I had thoughts of ending my life. That's why I sought out inpatient help.

I thought it would be an easy assignment to write out three traumatic events, and then other people would understand why I was so out of control – I was a victim of other people's cruelty.

So, I wrote out three major traumas by hand. I was supposed to read what I had written out loud to a peer from the facility. While I was waiting for her to meet up with me, I began to read over the "traumas" that I had written out. While reading, I realized something in one of the sentences wasn't entirely accurate. Then the following sentence didn't seem to be truthful, either. In fact, by the time my peer showed up, I had realized that I had "spun" a story out of a thread of truth and blown it out of proportion. Yes, I had been betrayed, but I had maximized and exaggerated the story until it was almost entirely a fabrication. I had believed my own distorted story. I had told it to other people, and they believed it, too. I didn't consider myself a liar, yet I believed the stories I had told so much that it caused me to hate the offender, hate life, and hate myself. I had used the exaggerations to justify and rationalize my unforgiveness, bitterness, and outrageous behavior. The pain of the initial betrayals grew as I embellished the truth, and I was literally out of my mind because of the distorted perception of the betrayal.

I realize now that the thread of truth where I was betrayed was also distorted by not understanding that the original trauma of betrayal began in childhood. I was reacting as an adult to past pain and trauma that kept part of me stuck at the emotional age where the original betrayal happened. I had been trapped at the initial point of pain, and when another betrayal occurred to me as an adult, there was a reaction instead of a response.

LACK OF BOUNDARIES = LACK OF SANITY

I had the TV on one day while I had a woman working with me at my house. The news showed a man in handcuffs being led by the police from his home. He was being arrested for raping a young child. My helper saw the footage of the man being walked to the police car and exclaimed, "Look at how the police are treating this man! That is so wrong!" What I saw was the police walking the man from his house. He was not being shoved or pushed around. He had surrendered. It looked peaceful to me. My other thought was, "Why are you so upset about him being arrested? Why aren't you thinking about the horrific act that he did to a child, possibly destroying the child's life? Why are you concerned about the rapist's rights? What about the child's rights?" She was reacting to the scene through the lens of her own pain and mistrust of authority. And so was I, but in a different way.

When I was a young teenager, I was sexually abused by a teacher. A family member found out about it, but she didn't call the police. She protected the pedophile and not me. Why? She had no boundaries. She had possibly been sexually violated as a child, and because of that, she had twisted thinking. She didn't want to "hurt" anyone. She thought that if she revealed his wrongdoing, she would be responsible for his downfall – the loss of his job or the loss of his reputation. She didn't understand that the abuser's actions would have been the cause of his own downfall.

People who were raised with no boundaries, or improper boundaries, will have a twisted sense of trust. When I was living apart from God, I would trust a man I'd never met before in a parking lot outside of a bar at three o'clock in the morning to buy a substance that could have killed me. At the same time, if a well-balanced, well-meaning person wanted to help me, I was suspicious of them. I called a help hotline one morning because I was seriously depressed and thought of ending my life. I was afraid to even give them my first name because I thought they might want to find me or follow me. At the time I was living in downtown Chicago. I was more afraid of the people who were set up to help me than the dangers of living in the city.

REFLECTIONS:

- Where in your life are you feeling DIScouragement or DISappointment, etc.? (See the list of DIS words in the Appendix.)
- Is there an area in your life where you hear yourself thinking or saying "all women" or "all men" or "all doctors," etc.?
- Do you have relationships in your life without boundaries? Sometimes relationships seem loving when in reality they are co-dependent or come from a sense of false responsibility or obligation.

ACTION STEPS:

Pay attention to negative thoughts and emotions. Recognize when the enemy is speaking to you, and replace those lies with the truth of what God says about you, others, or situations.

Recognize judgments and confess, forgive, and repent for making them. Be sure to forgive yourself.

3

BITTER ROOT JUDGMENTS & EXPECTATIONS

"See to it that no one falls short of the grace of God and that no bitter root grows up to cause trouble and defile many."
Hebrews 12:15 (NIV

Based on past experiences, mostly from childhood, I have learned that we have unconscious and subconscious thoughts and expectations that create cycles of hope or hurt. One day, I read the title of an email that said, "Judgments…The Greatest Freedom After Deliverance." I wasn't sure what a judgment was. The word judge can mean "to have as an opinion: guess or think." Well, I had opinions – lots of them – about almost everything and everyone. What's the problem with that, I wondered? Obviously, Jesus said there was a problem.

Matthew 7:1 says, *"Judge not, that you will not be judged."* I always wondered what that really meant. I knew that we were supposed to use judgment when making decisions and that there was a difference between good and bad judgment.

I'd never been taught about judgments in church, Bible studies, or even Bible College.

One day, I finally heard a woman say that the difference between good judgment and bad judgment *is the emotion associated with it.*

WHAT IS A BITTER ROOT JUDGMENT?

I have a friend named Brenda, and we met for lunch three to four times a week for about ten years. Brenda was usually late. I was not offended. It didn't bother me, or I wouldn't have continued meeting with her for ten years. I would sit in my car to catch up on emails or phone calls until she arrived or go into one of the little shops by the restaurants where we would eat. Yet, when it came to my mother, it was a different story. We had a horrible relationship since the day I was born, it seemed. When she was late to meet me, a negative emotion was tied to the judgment. "She's always late. She obviously has no respect for me or my time. She's only concerned about herself and never cared about me. Why would she start now? She's ruined my lunchtime and my day. She's so selfish and self-centered." That is called a bitter root judgment!

"See to it that no one falls short of the grace of God and that no bitter root grows up to cause trouble and defile many" (Hebrews 12:15).

WHAT IS A BITTER ROOT EXPECTATION?

I went to Toronto to a three-week school for leaders. I had a roommate, Edna, who was about fifteen years older than I was and well-schooled in inner healing and deliverance. I asked her a question one day.

"Do you think my mother and I will ever have a good relationship?"

Edna asked, "How old is your mother?" I told her she was seventy-five years old (I was fifty-seven at the time). She said, "Why don't you just learn to love her like she is?"

I burst into tears and ran from the room. I got alone and just sobbed and sobbed. I was surprised, and so was she, that I had such a childish reaction. All my life, I had waited for the mother God intended me to have to show up and love the little girl in my heart who needed her mom. I had an angry and contentious relationship with my mother; I believe the little girl inside me was angry and demanding the love and nurture she didn't get. Yet, I was not a little girl anymore. As an adult, I had a bitter root expectation that "she owed me." Whenever I saw her, I expected her to be rejecting, critical, and angry. In return, I became rejecting, critical, and angry.

I had to forgive my mother.

It didn't mean what happened to me was right or just, but as I forgave my mother, I began to heal. I repented for my bitter expectation for my mother to show up now and be the perfect mother for me, and I released her from my demands to nurture my heart. I gave her to Jesus, and I gave my little expectant heart to Him to love and nurture. As I let go of that bitter expectation, I immediately began to heal. For a week, I went through my remembrances looking for times when I had judged my mother for different things: for the way she was always on the phone (I was always on the phone), for the way she was always busy (I was always busy), for the way she was always angry (I was always angry), for the way she was always in a hurry (I was always in a hurry), for the way she was always late (I was always late), for the way she handled money (I didn't handle money well). I was just like her in every way that I had judged her and DIShonored her.

SOWING & REAPING CYCLES

Remember how harshly I judged my mother for being late for lunch? Soon afterward, I was going to meet my friend Janet. She was going to buy me a birthday lunch! How nice! I was looking forward to it. Yet, somehow, something came up. I got distracted, and suddenly, I was thirty minutes late. How disrespectful! (That's what I'd thought about Mom.) Janet was not pleased with me. She was hard on me. (I was hard on Mom.) She verbalized it and showed contempt for my disregard for her friendship and time. (I showed contempt and disregard for Mom.) I ruined our day. I was a problem, and she told me she would not do this again.

Unfortunately, the examples above are 100% true. When I attached a negative emotion to a judgment, it boomeranged back to me. Maybe I opened the door for the same behavior that I had judged so harshly to come back to me by the simple laws of sowing and reaping. I had judged, and now I was being judged. I judged others for the things I was blind to in myself.

JUDGMENTS KEEP YOU AND OTHERS IN BONDAGE

I had made negative judgments about my mother since I was a little girl. So, I began to repent of negatively and bitterly judging my mother for everything I could think of – her being so hard on me, her neglecting me, her rejecting me. I asked God to forgive me for judging her for being hard. I repented for being hard on myself, God, and my mother. I asked God to forgive me for dishonoring her, and by doing so, dishonoring God and myself. Ephesians 6:3 says, *"'Honor your father and mother,' which is the first commandment with promise, 'that it may be well with you and you may live long on the earth'"* (NKJV). I realized I wasn't honoring my mother. I renounced my agreements with the kingdom of darkness against her and asked the Holy Spirit to break the boomerang of the sowing and reaping cycle for my sin. I chose to bless my mother, honor her (not her actions, but her person and position as my parent), and honor God and the life He has given me.

I kept doing this for everything negative I could think of that I had judged my mother for. I even confessed, forgave, and repented of thoughts that a child of an unwed mother may have had. I may have rejected her because I felt that she rejected me. I may not have wanted her because I perceived she didn't want me. About two weeks later, I was leaving the leadership school in Toronto and heading home. My mother called and said, "Your Father wanted me to call you. He wants you to meet us at a restaurant by the airport when you land. He wants to see you." When she called me, she often said, "Your Father wanted me to call." I always interpreted it as, "I didn't want to call you, but your father . . . ." I resented that, but it was not "unexpected."

So, when I flew in, I immediately drove to the restaurant to see my parents. As we were sitting there and Dad was asking all about my trip, my mother turned to me and said, "I have been doing some thinking. I have been living my life my way, which hasn't worked well. I have decided to give my life back to Jesus."

WHAT? DID I HEAR THAT RIGHT?

She was sharing her heart with me about God. Wow!

For the next two weeks, I was highly motivated to continue confessing negative thoughts, words, and attitudes (bitter judgments) that I had made about my mother for over fifty-five years. One day, while driving, confessing, forgiving, repenting, and renouncing, I started to whine to Jesus. I said, "I feel like all I am doing is confessing, forgiving, repenting, and renouncing." I was basking in self-pity when I heard Jesus say, "I did the hard part." I immediately "saw" Him hanging on that cross because of me and for me. So, I continued to confess, forgive, repent, and renounce all agreements I could remember making with the kingdom of darkness.

One morning, very early, my mother called me. She didn't start with, "Your Father wanted me to call . . . ." She just said, "Good morning, Lynn." I asked if Dad was okay. She said he was. I asked her why she was calling. She said, "The Lord kept me up all night and showed me things I must ask you to forgive me for. I made life hard for you by____. Would you please forgive me?"

I said, "Of course, but the one thing you did that made you the best mother ever was you introduced me to Jesus Christ as a young child. For that, I am so grateful. Of all the mothers on the earth, I am grateful that He gave me you, Mom. I am sorry for all the trouble I gave you in life."

From that point on, our relationship began to be transformed. It wasn't great yet because we still had old habits of negative thinking, judging, and expecting the worst of each other. We had to learn how to love and respectfully relate. However, the biggest lesson I learned was that my mother was in bondage all of those decades because of *my* bitter judgments and expectations. My agreements with darkness kept us both bound up in pain. When I repented and changed my beliefs and received healing, my relationship with her and others was healed.

I went to visit my parents when my dad had some surgery. I was home with them for over a month. Mom and I walked in the park nearly every day. As we walked, some tension and irritation were still in the air. One day, we had a blowout . . . again. I gave her an ultimatum. Either she would have a relationship with me or with another person to whom she seemed to give priority over me. She got out of my car and said, "Goodbye." She had chosen the other person over her daughter again. My heart began to break again. However, this time, I gave the rejection, disappointment, and pain to Jesus. I get all I need from Him. I get love, nurture, acceptance, family, and everything from Him.

The next day, I called Mom and asked her to lunch. She said to pick her up when I was ready. I did. I had no bitterness towards her. We continued walking together until it was time for me to return to Tennessee. On my last day there, she said, "Please, don't leave now. We finally have a relationship for the first time in sixty years, and I don't want you to go. I love you." This is the relationship I had been longing for all my life, and so had she.

Now, we have what God had intended from the very beginning. We are reconciled to Him and each other. My mother and I occasionally discuss the shame she felt being pregnant out of wedlock. She brings it up – not me. She has explained that she "had" to get married to a man who rejected her because she got pregnant with me. My father loved me, but not her; he made that equally apparent. She retaliated against him for that by shunning, neglecting, and hating me. She hated herself. Now, she sees how she rejected me because of her own pain. I see my part, and she sees hers. Jesus has healed and is continuing to heal us.

REFLECTIONS:

- Ask the Lord if there is anyone in your life you have judged. Have you judged someone (like your mother/father) and now you recognize that you act just like them in the areas you judged them?
- Can you identify judgments that you made or may have made as a child against a parent, even in the womb?
- Ask the Lord if there is any person or circumstance in which you feel you have unfulfilled revenge in your heart that has turned into bitterness.
- In what area of your life do you feel you have a "right" to be offended?
- Do you have any anger or disappointment against God that caused you to judge Him?
- Do you judge yourself harshly? Do you have unrealistic expectations of yourself?
- Can you identify bitter expectations in your life? If it is about a parent, do you recognize that as dishonoring a parent and breaking a commandment?

ACTION STEPS:

When you see a pattern of behavior in yourself (that's not a positive thing), check your heart and ask God if it's because you judged someone else for a similar behavior.

Don't use the words "always" and "never" when thinking or speaking with a person in a negative way.

4

HOW JUDGMENTS AFFECT YOU

> *"Since each of you are part of God's family, never complain or grumble about each other so that judgment will not come on you, for the true Judge is near and very ready to appear!"*
> James 5:9 (TPT)

No one wants to be divorced from their own family. I had always perceived myself as a victim. That had been my identity, and I blamed my mother for it. I blamed my friends, I blamed boyfriends, my ex, or whatever the situation of the day was. As a result, I had strained relationships with my family and others. Today, I take responsibility for my own life and emotions. I am not a victim. Jesus has made a way for freedom from self-pity, blaming, and victimization.

I am not a child anymore and haven't been for decades. Yet, I was stuck in the past by my own bitter judgments and expectations while keeping others in pain with me. Hurt people hurt people. I hear so many people blaming their ex-spouses for the destruction of their lives and their relationship with their children. I believe bitterness and a desire to punish others for their problems are the only things standing in the way of true reconciliation and forgiveness. An identity of victimhood, unforgiveness, self-justification, rationalization, and bitterness is the self-centered hell that keeps us trapped and alienated from healthy relationships. There is finger-pointing and accusation coming from the pain, and that will never bring healing. Only taking 100% of the responsibility for our own emotions and responses will bring us healing. Life and hope return as we learn and bring Jesus into the equation.

ESAU SYNDROME

"Keep a sharp eye out for weeds of bitter DIScontent. A thistle or two gone to seed can ruin a whole garden in no time. Watch out for the Esau syndrome: trading away God's lifelong gift in order to satisfy a short-term appetite. You well know the story, how Esau later regretted that impulsive act and wanted God's blessing – but by then it was too late, tears or no tears" (Hebrews 12:14-17b, MSG).

One day, I had a discussion with my friend. Suddenly, I found myself getting a bit frustrated with her. What was up with her? About an hour later, I had a conversation with my attorney, and I didn't understand why he wasn't understanding what I was saying. I got so frustrated with him. What was up with him? Then, another BFF and I were talking, and I got frustrated with her! What was in the air? I drove home agitated. The following day, I drove forty-five minutes to meet a friend to look at some real estate. She called me and told me she would be forty-five minutes late. I tried not to be frustrated. I could get some gas for my car while I was waiting. My debit card was not working at the gas pump. I was incredibly frustrated again! Now, I am frustrated with a machine! Then I noticed that *I* was the common denominator in all situations where there was frustration in the last twenty-four hours.

I got into my car and searched for the word *frustration* in the dictionary on my phone: "2b: a deep, chronic sense or state of insecurity and dissatisfaction arising from unresolved problems or unfulfilled needs." Then I looked at the synonyms: *aggravating, exasperation, hassle, inconvenience, irk, peeve, pest, trial, vexation.*

The antidote is in the antonyms: *content, contentment, gratification, satisfaction.* I decided to shift my perspective. I said out loud, "I am grateful I have a debit card. I am grateful that there is money in the bank to buy gas. I am grateful that I have a car to put gas in. I am grateful that I have friends. I am content. I am satisfied, mostly because my God is good whether I have cash or not, a car or not, friends or not!"

The mind of God is content! Paul said that he "learned" to be content, whether shipwrecked, stoned, imprisoned, beaten, or starved (Philippians 4:11). I am grateful to be His today! I am thankful and satisfied with all of the blessings He has given me, including a sound mind, which I do not want to give away by thinking like the enemy again. By taking every thought, word, and attitude captive to be grateful, content, and appreciative, I see clearly, and I think like my Father. "This is a good day! Thank you, Lord!" I will not give away my life by living in the ways of hell (DIS). Instead, I will choose to focus and see what I do have instead of focusing on what I don't have.

I was never created to carry discontentment, dissatisfaction, or disagreeableness. It's not that now I agree with everyone about everything, but I don't need to add bitterness and ingratitude, which are the emotions that put blinders on me so that I cannot see what I have or what I am to do next.

RECOGNIZING CHILDISH WAYS

There was a woman in a group I was part of who was always running around while a speaker was talking, and it seemed she was constantly drawing attention to herself. She was very important to the group, but it appeared that she needed to prove her worth by buzzing around, distracting by "helping" while everyone else was quiet to listen to the speaker. It irritated me! I wanted to tell her to sit down and to stop whirling around and drawing attention to herself. Yet, time and time again, the same behavior would happen. Did anyone else notice? Or was it just me? I'm not sure. All I know is that it pushed my buttons.

But if I am dead to the flesh in Christ, I'm not supposed to have buttons. Dead people don't have buttons of offense. What about her behavior, real or imagined, was I judging with the mirror of my own heart?

Elbert Hubbard said, "We awaken in others the same attitude of mind we hold toward them." God showed me that I had never gotten approval from my mother as a child. I needed her encouragement and approval to mature in a healthy way. I needed encouragement and acceptance for brain development. What we don't get from our parents, we try to get in other ways, even negatively. I cried out for attention in many self-destructive ways before I received a lot of healing.

What I was judging that woman for I was actually doing in other ways. I was trying to get approval and acceptance from someone as an adult instead of getting healing love from the One who does encourage and approve of me. When I saw the same behavior in someone else, it triggered my pain. I was looking for those in authority over a ministry or business to give me encouragement and approval. I am not a child anymore, yet because of the lack in my childhood, I was still trying to get approval from outside of me in almost childish ways. Fishing for attention. Wanting or needing to be seen and wanting or needing to be heard. I didn't understand that because I "expected" the same disappointment that I had as a little girl, I was perceiving other people to behave (real or imagined) in the same way. I had a history of rejection, and now I subconsciously expected to be rejected, not approved of, or that people wouldn't be encouraging to me. People's behavior towards me was seen through the filter, the veil, the eyes of my wounded heart. Real or imagined, it was what I felt to be true.

So today, when someone is irritating me, I ask God where I am making a judgment. By getting to the root of the wounding, I see where it's idolatry for me to need someone else to affirm me. I can change my expectations by recognizing that as I pursue God, He has brought spiritual mothers, fathers, brothers, sisters, and children into my life to heal what my little broken heart did not receive in childhood. My mother didn't receive what she needed from her mother. My grandmother was an orphan and didn't know how to love, nurture and encourage. What was modeled or imprinted on us as children is what we understand as love until we learn to receive approval, encouragement, and acceptance from Jesus Christ.

EXPECTATIONS CAN BE SELF-FULFILLING PROPHECIES

Once I attended a church full of young people. They did a video presentation of what they were going to be doing over the holidays. One of the girls in the video said, "I'm going to my mother's house, and my entire family will come over. My uncle always gets drunk and picks a fight with my other uncle, and pretty soon the whole family is fighting. It happens every year." Everybody laughed. She expected this every year, and the people were laughing, not because it's funny, but because they can relate and have their own expectations. Unfortunately, it's a bitter root expectation, as referred to in Hebrews 12:15: *"See to it that no one fall short of the grace of God and that no bitter root grows up to cause trouble and defile many"* (NIV).

Basically, what she was doing was unknowingly empowering the kingdom of darkness. The power of life and death is in the power of the tongue, and by this, many were defiled.

I used to be in the habit of expecting everything I did to go wrong. I had a saying, "Blessed is he who expects nothing, for they shall not be disappointed." I was using my words and expectations to curse myself and create self-fulfilling prophecies. Now I know that I was making agreements with the kingdom of darkness, giving my authority and power to it and bringing disappointment and trauma into my life.

I was planning a trip to a conference. Someone in my family lived in the same state but in a different city known for being expensive. I told a friend I would visit my relative while I was on my way to the event. Yet I heard myself saying, "Watch me fly all the way there, book an expensive hotel, and at the last minute, my relative tell me that she had something important come up that she had to attend to and not be available to meet with me after all."

My friend asked me, "Is that a bitter root expectation?"

Oddly, we both burst out laughing! I had just unintentionally made a prophetic agreement with the kingdom of darkness with my words and expectations. I immediately renounced that agreement and made another expectant declaration. "My relative and I will have the time of our lives together when I visit her! We will have joy and love overflowing as we live in the blessing God created our family to be." Guess what? We had such a beautiful time together. I have such fond memories of that visit. I love her, and I won't forget the joy and love we experienced.

What changed? Have others changed, or have the words of my mouth and my expectations changed? Because whether real or imagined, we will create what we are expecting.

JUDGMENTS AGAINST PARENTS SET YOU UP FOR FAILURE

John and Paula Sanford are pioneers of inner healing and deliverance ministries and the founders of Elijah House. They teach that, "Anytime anyone has any issue whatsoever, it ALWAYS goes back to dishonoring a mother or father." When I first heard this teaching, I rewound it and listened to it over and over. I couldn't be hearing that correctly, could I?

Then, I was having difficulty with a business partner who had been misappropriating dividends to himself. I had to decide whether to take him to court, which could be drawn out and expensive, or to let a substantial amount of money go. I asked the Lord where I may have opened the door to financial problems. I started thinking about what John and Paula Sanford had said about dishonoring a mother or father. I began asking God to forgive me for judging the way my mother had handled her money. While I had forgiven my mother for a number of things already, I realized I had criticized her for that, too, at least in my heart. I also asked God to forgive me for judging my dad for being oblivious and ignoring his money and where it was going. I also repented for dishonoring both of them by having bitter judgments about their use and handling of their money. I shed tears over this as I understood the damage I had done to them and myself by being critical and judgmental.

As I repented, I did not know that within thirty-six hours, my business partner would email me asking how much he owed me. He paid me back in full that week! That is the power of following God's ways.

Leviticus 20:9 says in the Amplified Bible, *"If anyone curses his father or mother, he shall most certainly be put to death; he has cursed his father or mother; his blood is on him (that is, he bears full responsibility for the consequences)."* In Proverbs 30:17, it says, *"The eye that mocks his father and dishonors his elderly mother deserves to be plucked out by the ravens of the valley and fed to the young vultures,"* and Proverbs 20:20 says, *"Whoever curses his father or mother – his lamp will go out in deep darkness."* I think God was serious about honoring our parents!

LET'S TAKE THIS CONCEPT FARTHER

Not recognizing the judgments you have made against a parent can cause your heart to perceive your husband or wife as the unhealed, unrepentant image of your parent. Real or imagined, your spouse will be perceived through the judgments you made towards your parent.

God will send you opportunities to recognize and work out these issues in your heart. When you find yourself comparing someone to your parent, it's important to recognize that it might not be that person who is the problem or issue. It could be the way you view them because of your unresolved issues. *"Guard your heart above all else, for it determines the course of your life"* (Proverbs 4:23, NLT).

JUDGMENTS AGAINST YOURSELF

I was at a meeting for leaders, and the leader of the meeting said that if we wanted prayer for a deeper compassion for people, come forward and get prayer from Rebecca. The leader said Rebecca had the greatest gift of compassion they'd ever seen on anyone. Immediately I was skeptical. When I was growing up, compassion and mercy were seen as weaknesses. I grew up in an environment of criticism and put-downs that my family believed would encourage me to try harder and inspire me to do my best. Well, of course, that's not what it did. As a child, I accepted those criticisms as truth because it was from the adult who was put there by God to encourage and love me. It caused a type of trauma from lack of love, lack of nurture, lack of encouragement, and a lack of seeing the delight in somebody's eyes when you walk in a room. Children need that because it actually helps the prefrontal cortex develop. Without that, the adult center of your brain is impaired.

I went forward to have Rebecca pray for me, even though I was skeptical. She was quiet because she was listening to God before praying for me. And then she said, "God wants you to have compassion on yourself, for yourself." And that's all she said. She prayed into that.

I went back to my seat thinking, "I don't know what she's talking about." I was expecting something much better than that from her. I kept thinking about it in my mind. A few days later, I was backing out of the garage. There are three buttons on my remote visor to put the garage door down, and I hit the wrong button. I heard myself saying in my head, "Oh, come on, dummy. It's only three buttons. It's the same one every time. And you missed it again." I don't think I'll ever forget that moment because I became aware of what Proverbs 4:23 means when it says to pay attention to my innermost being because from there flows all the issues of life. I was being critical of myself instead of having compassion for myself, just as Rebecca had prayed.

One day when I was carrying in a bag of groceries, I dropped something, and I heard myself saying, "Come on, dummy. Pick it up. Seriously. Can't you get the groceries in the house?" I was aware of Matthew 22:37, when Jesus said, *"Love the Lord your God with all your heart, all your mind."* The Passion translation says *". . . with all your thoughts, all the emotions, all that's within you. And then love neighbors as you love yourself."* I would add, "or love others as you love yourself." It doesn't sound like love to call myself an idiot. It doesn't sound like love to condemn, judge, criticize, and insult myself. When I began to pay attention, I realized I'd been judging myself harshly.

One day I was standing in an airport, and there was a very, very long line for coffee. People were getting ready to board their early morning flights, and the line for coffee was going slowly. There was a young mother with about an eight-year-old boy standing in line behind me. I felt sorry for the kid because as much as I didn't like standing there for all the time we'd been standing in line, I was sure he liked it even less because he didn't even want coffee. All of a sudden, the boy broke the line and said, "Daddy!" He saw his father coming down the concourse. He ran past me, and right in front of his dad and everybody in that line, he tripped and hit the concourse floor extremely hard. Everybody in the whole line cringed because they heard when his little body hit that hard pavement.

What I saw next was his dad reach down, gently help his son up, and hold him close to him. He just kind of held him quietly as he said, "Are you all right, son?" His son didn't move. He just sat in his father's arms.

Watching this, I had this thought occur to me. If that had been me as a little girl running, and I tripped, I would have heard in my own mind, "Are you kidding me? You've been walking for about seven or eight years now, and you still can't walk? And on top of that, you not only fall, but you fall in front of all these people, embarrassing and humiliating yourself. I don't know why you bother to keep on trying to walk. Why don't you just cut your legs off? You're obviously a failure. Why don't you just quit trying?" And it dawned on me, that's how I speak to myself. I got that imprinting from people who also spoke to themselves that way. It was blocking my ability to receive love, to forgive myself, and to not judge, condemn, or criticize myself. I needed to lighten up on myself.

Perfectionism is a twisted way of thinking. I began to notice that I was hyper-sensitive to any form of failure in myself. Maybe that's a form of pride. Maybe I think I know better than God. There's another perspective to have when I make mistakes and what looks like a failure: I can see it as an opportunity. You can't fail if you don't give up. You can learn from what you missed that made it look like a failure. God sees through our failures. Love covers a multitude of sins. He's not surprised by our failures, so why should we be? The greatest people in world history have failed multiple times, but they kept getting up.

BOOMERANG RESENTMENT & UNFORGIVENESS

Have you ever tried to forgive someone? You know you're supposed to forgive them. You even want to forgive them, but they keep coming back in your memory with reoccurring feelings of unforgiveness and bitterness. Something that I've learned is that our forgiveness affects how we view others and ourselves.

There was a woman, I'll call her Sue, who was supposed to be speaking with a group of people I connected her with. One day, Sue told me she had shared with the group that I was lying about certain qualifications I had in a business I was part of. I said, "You told them what?" I couldn't believe she would actually do something like that, let alone tell me about it when she knew she had lied about me. Truthfully, it was so outrageous that I did not believe her, but when I asked one of the people in the group, they confirmed what she had said. I sought help from the people over her in leadership, but when they confronted her, she denied it.

I could not believe what was going on. I was being looked at as a liar because I knew the people in the group would assume that a leader would tell the truth. It was especially frustrating because I had established relationships with these people. The group's reputation in our community was built on trust. I was furious.

The leadership of the organization sent out an email explaining there had been a misunderstanding and a miscommunication. That brought me some peace, so I tried to forgive Sue. I chose to forgive her, and I blessed her. Then the next thing I knew, I was having recurring, tormenting anger and resentment against her. The thoughts were going around in my mind, and they wouldn't stop. I began having dreams and nightmares about the whole situation, and I could not get rid of these thoughts. They were preoccupying my mind when I needed to focus on other things, and I could not understand why I could not let it go when I needed and wanted to. I called a mentor of mine and asked for help. She said these life-changing words to me. "Break off any judgment that she made against you and break off any judgments you made against her."

So, I did. I said, "Father, in the name of Jesus Christ, I forgive Sue for judging me as disqualified. As having no integrity. As being dishonest. As being a liar and a cheat. I forgive her, and I break off the negative judgments spoken against me in the name of Jesus Christ. And Father, I also ask you to forgive me for where I judged her for being a liar, for being arrogant, for being deceitful, for being undermining. In

Jesus' name, I renounce and break those agreements I made with the kingdom of darkness, in the name of Jesus Christ. And I speak peace over her. I speak blessings over her. I speak life over her in Jesus' name."

It wasn't long before I was invited to a small gathering at a friend's house, and Sue was there. I sat next to her, and I didn't think at all about the previous wounding and betrayal that I had felt. It never occurred to me. I didn't even notice until I was driving home. There is freedom and there is healing in Jesus' name.

I've learned to change my inner dialogue. I've learned to meditate on scriptures like, *"And I will give you a new heart, and I will put a new spirit in you. I will take out your stony, stubborn heart and give you a tender, responsive heart"* (Ezekiel 36:26, NLT). I have to apply that to myself, not just to other people. I can only love you with a love I have for myself, and if the reflection of my heart is bitter, hard, or critical towards me, I can only give you what I have. It says in Psalm 34:12-14, *"Whoever of you loves life and desires to see many good days, keep your tongue from evil and your lips from telling lies. Turn from evil and do good; seek peace and pursue it."* Now I pay attention to my innermost being, for from there flows all the issues of life (Proverbs 4:23).

What's your issue? I suggest using scripture to build Godly strongholds of love, hope, and peace. Meditate on, recite, contemplate, and declare what God says, which is truth. Don't focus on what society says, or what your family has said, or what teachers have said. Forgive those who spoke those things over you, and bless them because they said those same things about themselves. Psalm 119:165 says,*"There is such a great peace and well-being that comes to the lovers of your Word, and they will never be offended"* (TPT).

I asked God to forgive me for any place that I accepted the lies – the hard, sharp, critical, condemning, judging words –

and then made them my own and believed them. I renounced and broke every agreement I made with them, and I asked God to heal my heart. I returned to the stronghold of love because I'm a prisoner of hope as Zechariah 9:12 says, and that's where my authentic self is. It's in the nature of my Father, the King of Kings.

I read once that Jesus was a stranger to self-hate. The religious spirit has a voice that says you're not good enough, and that you should be ashamed of yourself. It says that if people knew what you really were like, you would not be accepted. How can you call yourself a Christian? The truth is that none of us are perfect. Even in the Bible, Noah was a drunk. David was a murderer. The twelve disciples were not picked because they were perfect. They were picked as an example of humanity, and just like me and you, God can use the foolish to confound the wise. He didn't make junk. I'm created in the nature and the image of my Father, and I choose to have Godly thoughts towards me and towards you, removing all elements of hostility.

Recently I was in the office with my mom, and I asked her if I could help her with the books because she seemed to be struggling. She said, "No, you're too stupid, too." Instead of that breaking my heart for me, as an adult, it broke my heart for her because I realized that she thinks that way about herself. So all she could give me was what she had, which was a hard heart towards herself. Instead, I forgave my mom.

Life is about choices, and I choose to tear down the thoughts that are in agreement with the kingdom of darkness and overcome them using the word of God, which is the Spirit of Truth.

Choose who you want to believe.

Choose wisely, and choose now, keeping firm in your resolve. No matter what it looks like on the outside, keep going after God and what He says in His Word. If God says it, choose to believe it, meditate on it, think about it, declare it, and believe it until it happens.

The Word of God is a hammer, a fire, and a sword, and it will tear down the lies of the kingdom of darkness every time – if you don't quit.

I've learned to be thankful that I'm not where I used to be, to appreciate who and what God has put in my life to transform me, and to know He's not going to leave me as He found me. As long as I'm walking with Him and living in His ways, my life is increasingly transformed. The people who used to point at me on the street and tell their kids not to talk to people like me now send their kids to me because I found a better way, the way of love. If God can do this for me, imagine what He can do for you.

REFLECTIONS:
- Do you feel like you're a victim of someone or something?
- Is there unforgiveness or judgment in your heart in the form of self pity, bitterness, or self-hate?
- Do you get stuck in self pity?
- Do you recognize where you may have dishonored a parent even in your thoughts or as a child from the womb until the present day?
- Do you find yourself frustrated often?
- Is there someone you find yourself repeatedly trying to forgive?
- What judgment did you make against them? What judgement do you feel they made or said against you? (See appendix for prayers to break off judgments.)

ACTION STEPS:

Consider some ways to practice contentment, gratitude, satisfaction, and thankfulness.

Who are the people God has placed in your life in the last five years to help you grow and heal?

What five things has God done for you in the last five years that touched your heart and gave you a testimony?

5

ATTITUDES ARE INDICATORS

A scoffer seeks Wisdom in vain (for his very attitude blinds and deafens him to it), but knowledge is easy to him who (being teachable) understands."
Proverbs 14:6 (AMPC)

In his book *The Strangest Secret*, radio personality and motivational speaker Earl Nightingale suggested that attitude is a magic word because it can either bring us success or failure. One thing's for sure, we are 100% responsible for our attitudes. We can't blame our attitudes on someone else. One time a friend of mine shared with me that when he complained to God that a certain person made him have a bad attitude, God told him that the person just revealed to him an attitude he already had. It wasn't the other person causing the attitude; that person just brought that attitude to light.

My mom used to tell me not to hang out with certain kids in our neighborhood because they had bad attitudes. It seemed like those were the kids who were always getting in trouble. When I had a bad attitude, I was sent to my room until I could have a better attitude. Bill Johnson, a well-known author, speaker, and senior leader of Bethel Church in Redding, California, says that when he and his wife were raising their kids, they didn't focus much on behavior. They corrected the attitude, and then the negative behavior didn't happen.

When I have a negative attitude or outlook on a situation, it changes my perception. I cannot see the solution; I only see the problem, and I lose hope. I see the glass as half-empty instead of my cup running over. I have learned to "reframe" my thinking and my attitude. When I have a situation that seems to be difficult, I change my perspective and say, "This isn't happening to me. This is happening for me. I don't have to do this; I get to do this." Now, I'm seeing the problem through the eyes of the Lord.

When I looked up the word attitude in the dictionary, it said to see more at *APTITUDE*. There is a direct correlation between attitude and aptitude. When I was growing up, there were a bunch of kids in my class who started saying that they hated math. I wanted to fit in, so I said I hated math. I didn't have an opinion before then about math, nor did I realize that the people who hated math usually had bad scores. Once I started saying I hated math, I began struggling with math. I remember my mother trying to work with me. I am still healing from that! And then, in third grade, I sat next to twin boys. They were cute! When it was time for math, they would always say, "We love math!" Well, I had a crush on them. I started saying that I loved math, too! After that, my math scores were so high that I was in high school math while I was still in middle school. It was easy for me! My attitude changed, so my aptitude changed, and my difficulties in that subject were over. It wasn't because I had a better teacher; it was because I had a better attitude.

Neuroscience proves that it takes four hundred repetitions to build a new neural pathway in the brain, UNLESS you do it in joy. Then it only takes twelve repetitions to build a new neural pathway. That's a huge difference! Deuteronomy 28:47a says: *"Because you did not serve the Lord, your God, with joyfulness of (mind and) heart (in gratitude) for the abundance of all (with which he has blessed you), therefore, you will serve your enemies . . . "* (AMPC). One of the reasons we may find ourselves serving our enemies is because we are blind; we are not perceiving they are taking us over because we have a bad attitude. We function poorly, cursing ourselves. We can't see that we are our own worst enemy. We can't see a solution because now our perceptions are distorted. We were never created to carry negativity. We were only created to carry love and hope, peace and joy. John N. Mitchell says, "Our attitude toward life determines life's attitude toward us."

Our attitudes and then the words we speak reveal our hearts. Proverbs 4:23 says, *"Pay attention to your innermost being, for from there flow all the issues of life."* When I pay attention, notice, and become aware of my innermost thoughts and feelings and then hear my own words, I can either hear love and peace or fear and bitterness. This brings conviction, not condemnation. It brings the negative to the cross, and I can then choose to confess, forgive, repent, and bless the people or organizations that I "perceive" (either real or imagined) have hurt me. I have been hurt by well-meaning people and also some not-so-well-meaning people. I developed unforgiveness, which created an attitude of bitterness and blindness, thereby distorting my perceptions of myself and others.

ANTIDOTES

An attitude of GRATITUDE: When we are the most "lost," gratitude is our North Star. We must shift our focus and perspective to be grateful for what we do have and not focus on the perceived "lack" in our life. We must make it a habit first thing in the morning to be grateful and list, acknowledge, and recognize what we do have. For instance, water is a gift from a gracious God! I have been in Pemba, Mozambique, during a drought when the entire city ran out of water. Where there is no water, there's no life. It is huge! So, I'm thankful for water, and that helps me focus on what I do have.

An attitude of APPRECIATION: What we focus on will grow in our perceptions. What I behold, I become. I read once that when we meditate on gratitude for at least ten minutes a day, it boosts our immune system fifty percent. I recommend making a list of ten things that the Lord and other people have done for you over the last five to ten years. Recognize the people who have helped you in life. I have had loyal, trustworthy friends, leaders, mentors, and wise counsel all through my journey with God. As I learned to forgive, I saw my mother and the generational blessings she carries that I inherited from her. She always cared for the poor. She always found great real estate deals and made a business out of them serving "the least of these." She had a great eye for décor. She was a hard worker and a good example of taking responsibility for your own home and the community.

An attitude of THANKFULNESS: I like these lyrics to a song, "Thank Him in the beginning, thank Him in the middle, thank Him in the end." There were ten lepers Jesus healed. Only one came back to thank Jesus, and he was the only one who was made "whole." Thankfulness brings us wholeness in body, soul, and spirit.

FILTERS WE SEE THROUGH

I can see through what I think, what I want, or what I feel. If I think I'm ugly, I will see myself as ugly. If I want something so badly that I want it more than what God wants for me, I will see through the filter of self-will and rebellion. If I "feel" like you're angry, then you may mirror my attitude or my emotions. If I think I am rejected, I will see God and others rejecting me, either real or imagined. I will believe and expect rejection all around me. If I see through my past pain, I live with the lie that if my mother rejects me, all women will reject me. I came into agreement with that lie and judgment in my childhood, or maybe, in the womb. It became my PERCEIVED reality.

> **If I think I can do something, I can.**
> **If I think I can't do something, I can't.**
> **I am "right" if I think I can or if I think I can't.**

I may be "right" in my perception, but that does not make it true.

A couple of months after I submitted my life back to the Lord, I ran into a woman who was friends with my mother when I was growing up. She had a healing room, and she invited me to visit. She also had different gatherings with women where there was teaching and prayer. I went to one of the gatherings and asked her to pray for me. She asked me what I wanted prayer for, and I told her that I was bipolar and had many other mental disorders. She said, "No, you don't."

I was confused by that statement, as the doctors said that I was bipolar, that I had an eating disorder, borderline personality disorder, addiction, and suicidal tendencies. I told her that. She said, "You've been lied to." Then she said, "You are the head, not the tail; you are above and not beneath. You have the mind of Christ. You were formed by Him in your mother's womb. You are fearfully and wonderfully made." Then she prayed for me. I was baffled.

At the next meeting, I asked for prayer again. She asked me, "What do you want prayer for?" I said, "I'm bipolar, bulimic, addicted, and have borderline personality disorder."

She said, "No you don't. You've been lied to."

I got frustrated and said, "The doctors in Florida, the doctors in Illinois, and the doctors in Texas did not all get together and conspire to lie to me. How can you say that?"

She told me there are facts and there is truth. Those are different things. The facts are that I have symptoms of bipolar, etc., but the truth is I have the mind of Christ. I was created in His image, and He is *not* bipolar, addicted, and so on. It's on earth as it is in heaven.

This woman explained further. "Choose who you want to believe," she said. "You are the head and not the tail, above and not beneath. You are the apple of His eye. You are loved. His plans are for you, to give you a hope and a future. His thoughts for you are more than the sands of the sea. You are created in His image. Choose who you want to believe. The doctors or God?"

She invited me to come to the healing room and to renounce and break the agreements that I had made with the lies and the father of lies, Satan. I began my journey of learning the ways of God to heal and deliver through confession, forgiveness, repentance, renouncement, and receiving His Love and His Truth.

Our thinking patterns or thinking habits either agree with God or they don't. If we have the Word of God and the mind of Christ, we know that He is the Word, and we must choose to think His thoughts by meditating on Truth.

Proverbs 23:7 (AMP) says, *"For as he thinks in his heart, so is he (in behavior – the one who manipulates)."*

If I want something badly (for example: a house, a car, or something that can be an idol), it's easy to convince myself that God told me I could have it. I know a woman who wanted a husband so badly that when she was contacted by a man in Nigeria who told her that he was in love with her, she believed him. He wanted her to send him $10,000. He was going to open an orphanage and then send for her to come and marry him. They would live in Nigeria running the orphanage together. She wanted a man so badly that he became an idol, and she heard "God" tell her to do what the man in Nigeria was suggesting. I do believe she heard a god, but not the God who died for her. The desire to have a man was a deep longing to be loved that she hadn't learned to receive from the God of love. Instead, she began looking for "love" outside of herself, and she paid a price for it.

I used to think that when I got what I wanted, then I'd be happy. I was always wanting something on the outside of me to make me happy. There is nothing outside of me that will ever fill the place God put in us for Him. Nothing else will ever satisfy us for long. Idols always fail. Maybe when I get the "right" man, I will be happy. Maybe when I get the "right" house, the "right" job, and the "right" car, then I will be happy. When that doesn't satisfy me anymore, maybe I chose the "wrong" man and I will look for another. Maybe I chose the "wrong" job, the "wrong" city, etc. Pretty soon, life becomes hopeless because there is nothing outside of us that can satisfy us without God and His ways.

Relying on feelings is like allowing an impulsive three-year-old child to run my life. My feelings can mislead me. Maybe I don't "feel" like going to work today. I "feel" like eating the whole pie. I "feel" like you owe me. If I follow my feelings, they, too, can become an idol. I cannot follow my feelings; I have to follow Jesus. I don't get to feed the impulsive feelings of doing what I want, when I want to, and how I want to. There are boundaries in every area of life, and they are there for a reason. I could feel like driving eighty miles an hour, yet there will be consequences for doing so. I could feel like eating the whole pie and only pie for every meal, but there would be consequences. I choose to exercise whether I feel like it or not. I choose to discipline myself when I feel like buying another pair of shoes that I don't need or can't afford.

I have the choice to live impulsively or intentionally. Purposeless people are usually dissatisfied with regular life and look for something – anything – to fill the void. The feeling of having no worth or value can lead to medicating with something – anything – outside of us. God wants us to live with intention. In Habakkuk 2:2, it says to *"write the vision and make it plain on tablets,"* and in Psalm 139:16 (HCSB), it says, *"Your eyes saw me when I was formless; all my days were written in Your book and planned before a single one of them began."* Our desire should be to align ourselves with the plans that were designed for us before we were ever formed in our mothers' wombs. There is no lasting satisfaction outside of that. We get to seek God and keep inquiring until we know the bigger picture of what is written in our DNA. On judgment day, we will answer for what we were called to do, so we need to seek that plan and walk it out. If not, we will perceive that God has let us down. The book of Proverbs talks about drifters, wayward and wandering people. One of the greatest deceptions from the enemy is to think we have all the time in the world, but we do not want to end up at the end of our lives and realize that we have blown past our destiny.

"Not that I am implying that I was in any personal want, for I have LEARNED how to be CONTENT (satisfied to the point where I am not disturbed or disquieted) in whatever state I am. I know how to be abased and live humbly in straitened circumstances, and I know also how to enjoy plenty and live in abundance. I have learned in any circumstances the secret of facing every situation, whether well-fed or going hungry, having a sufficiency and enough to spare or going without and being in want" (Philippians 4:11-12, AMPC).

To walk in clarity, we need to learn to abide, dwell, and inhabit His ways, His nature, and His character.

REFLECTIONS:

- Do you recognize any negative attitudes in your life?
- Do you get frustrated easily or often?
- Where do you catch yourself in a negative attitude and shift your focus to what you DO have to be grateful for?
- Can you see where attitudes may reveal unforgiveness and/or judgments in your heart?

ACTION STEPS:

Start a daily gratitude list of five things you do have.

Create a habit of remaining content.

Ask God how you can grow in attitudes of humility, patience, gentleness, and meekness.

Find scriptures to meditate, recite, contemplate and declare.

6

RESPOND OR REACT?

"'If you understand what I'm saying, you need to respond!'
Then he said to them, 'Be diligent to understand the meaning behind
everything you hear, for as you do, more understanding will be given
to you. And according to your longing to understand, much more will
be added to you. Those who listen with open hearts will receive more
revelation. But those who don't listen with open hearts will lose what
little they think they have!'"
Mark 4:23-25 (TPT)

When I have an exaggerated reaction to something or someone, the question I ask myself is, "Where else have I experienced this in my life?" Most of the time, it didn't start with my current situation. I look for similarities from my past. Does this remind me of an experience I've had before? Maybe I've created a place of protection around myself from past pain, and now it's a stronghold. A lot of times my reactions come from family origins. Maybe I think my friend is rejecting me because my dad treated me the same way. So, I need to forgive my dad, and I need to ask God to forgive me for reacting that way. Maybe someone says something to me, and it sounds like my mother, but I don't realize that in the moment. It seems like the problem is new or the situation is new. Afterward, I can look back and see that I am reacting like I would to my mother.

I heard a saying once: "I'm only responsible for what I say, not for what you hear." There is a spirit that twists communication and causes misunderstandings. It wants me to hear you say, "You look terrible in that hat," even if you didn't say anything negative. The antidote for that is, "Love believes the best." If someone insists they didn't say something you thought they did, believe the best of that person and assume it was a misunderstanding. Don't allow the enemy to twist your communication and cause division.

These days, I pray to understand rather than to be understood, but that is a new habit. When I first came into Christianity, I was attending a church in my hometown. Then I learned there was something called prophecy and that the Bible says, "All y'all prophesy." I asked the pastor of my church if he would teach me about prophecy. He said, "Well, you know, not quite everybody prophesies." I told him I'd been reading that everybody prophesies. He said, "Why don't you teach that at your house, Lynn." Great idea. At the time, I didn't take offense.

Soon afterward, I learned of another church that had a school where they taught that everyone could prophesy, so I started attending there. They also taught how to pray for the sick and how to equip the saints. It was more than just sitting on the pew and being quiet. Later, I went to a city prayer meeting and saw the pastor from my former church. He said, "Lynn, I want to introduce you to our missionary from India. Ravi, this is our friend Lynn. She used to come to our church until she got too spiritual for us." I was shocked into silence, which for me is a miracle!

Four or five days later, I called that pastor. I told him I didn't stop going to his church because I believed I was too spiritual for them.

He said, "What are you talking about?"

I said, "When you introduced me to Ravi, you said I quit going to your church because I got too spiritual for you." He assured me he never said that. I was confused because that is what I heard, but rather than hold it against him, I said, "I believe you. I'm sorry. I misheard that." At the time, I was doing an internship with Patricia King, and she told me the reason I said that was because love believes the best. In the end, it didn't matter who was right. It mattered that there wasn't enmity between brothers and sisters in Christ.

Years ago, I was at a missions base in Texas. It was the last week of the six-week training, and we had one free day to do laundry and other errands for the week. My 26-year-old friend was driving back home with me the following weekend. It was a thirteen-hour drive. I called him and asked him to come with me to get an oil change for the car and do laundry so we'd be ready to leave when the weekend came. He told me no. He explained that he'd recently been off-base with another woman from the training and was told not to be out with a member of the opposite sex.

I said, "I am not a 24-year-old woman. I am older than your mother. Get in the car and let's go."

He still said no. He didn't want to get in trouble and risk not graduating.

I was FURIOUS! I got into the car and headed to the oil change business. I was driving fast and furious. I called a friend in Colorado to express my rage. She said, "It sounds like you're offended."

I said, "You think? Do they think I'm a pedophile or something? This reminds me of when I was in sixth grade and my mother accused me of being sexually inappropriate with a boy from the neighborhood . . . oh my gosh!" I realized I was reacting to my mother's hurtful accusation that happened about forty-five years earlier. I sat in front of the laundromat and confessed, forgave, repented, and asked the Lord to heal my heart from the pain. My reaction was extreme and exaggerated. No one else at that missions base was upset or disturbed in any way over the rule except for me.

When you go up to someone and pat them on the back, they usually turn towards you and respond in the same manner that you are relating to them – unless they have sunburned skin. In that case, they may jump out of their chair and react to the pain. You didn't cause the source of their pain, but until it heals, everyone who touches them will see that pain come out towards them.

My pain came out in distorted ways, like addiction, anger, self-hatred, and blaming others. I had no understanding of where the pain came from or how to heal. The world says, "Get over it," or, "Time heals all wounds." This is not true. Only Jesus heals. Only by recognizing the roots of our pain, applying God's solutions of forgiveness, and taking responsibility for our problems will we mature and heal.

Thought patterns are habits. Attitudes are habit-forming. Drama and trauma can be addictive. Emotions can be habit-forming and addictive. Even negative emotions release dopamine, which can lead to addiction. We tend to be addicted to the behaviors and reactions from childhood instead of renewing our minds and restoring sanity. Emotions may begin as a "normal" response, but if they are allowed to go unchecked, they can bring us to a place of fear and self-protection instead of allowing God to protect us. We love the negative emotions because we falsely believe they are working for us. But, like everything false, they will quickly quit working for us and rob us of life and hope. I heard Joyce Meyers once say, "I never knew how I was going to feel any given day until Satan told me." Then she said, "Now I don't follow my feelings. I follow the truth. I follow Jesus."

I don't have to be right. Jesus didn't come to the earth to be right, or to give us rights. He submitted Himself to the Father and to the ones the Father had given to Him. He allowed love to cover a multitude of sins (1 Peter 4:8). It's always going to be about Him and His will to form our character. It's about being humble. It's about being meek. It's about sharing truth. It's about looking like love, and love doesn't look like controlling, rejecting, rebelling, insulting, or criticizing.

One of the daily declarations I make is, "I don't judge, I'm not judged. I don't condemn, I'm not condemned. I don't criticize, I'm not criticized." When I am judged or criticized, it is an opportunity for me to grow in maturity because God uses it to form my character. As it says in Colossians 3:12-14: *"You are always and dearly loved by God! So robe yourself with virtues of God, since you have been divinely chosen to be holy. Be merciful as you endeavor to understand others, and be compassionate, showing kindness toward all. Be gentle and humble, unoffendable in your patience with others. Tolerate the weaknesses of those in the family of faith, forgiving one another in the same way you have been graciously forgiven by Jesus Christ. If you find fault with someone, release this same gift of forgiveness to them. For love is supreme and must flow through each of these virtues. Love becomes the mark of true maturity"* (TPT).

When we walk in love, it looks like the fruit of the Spirit. It looks like joy, peace, patience, kindness, goodness, gentleness, long-suffering, and self-control. It looks like the Beatitudes. Love is where we are called to abide, to remain in, to dwell in. Love is walking in the Spirit and not in the flesh.

The principle of sowing and reaping comes into play here. If I want kindness, I need to show kindness. If I want friends, I need to be friendly. If I want love, I must be loving. When something happens that I think is unjust, I look for where I have sown injustice. If I don't like what's coming against me, I check to see where it could be my responsibility. Where have I thrown out those words? Did I complain to a friend and say, "I'll never let that person do that to me again." Did I make an inner vow that built a cage and a wall around my heart to protect myself? Jesus didn't die for our self-protection. He's our Protector.

Proverbs 14:6 in the Amplified Bible says, *"A scoffer –* that's somebody with an attitude, right? – *seeks wisdom in vain for his very attitude blinds and deafens him to it. But knowledge is easy to him, being teachable, who understands."* Knowledge comes easily to the person who has understanding. Proverbs 4:5 says, *"Get Godly wisdom, and with wisdom, get understanding."*

I used to say, "God, you said, 'If anyone lacks wisdom, let him ask.' Well, I've been asking for wisdom. What seems to be the problem?"

And He said, "I've given you wisdom, you just haven't applied it."

I've learned how to apply it now by taking every thought captive that does not identify with God. How do I change my thoughts? By meditating on the Word. I do not allow the passion of my emotions to cause me to sin (Ephesians 4:29, TPT). I can be passionate, but it's not always a Godly passion. Sometimes my emotions can come out sideways. So, I have changed my thought habits by meditating on the Word. There is nothing more powerful than the Word. It's a sword. It's a hammer. It's fire, like it says in Jeremiah 23:29. When I've had strongholds of behavior, I tear them down using the Word, and then I build Godly strongholds. One of the ways I do this is by personalizing scripture. It helps me to make declarations. Sometimes I set reminders in my phone, like, "I'm a channel through which God's love, power, wisdom, compassion, tenderness, and wealth flow ceaselessly, copiously, and endlessly."

I have to get rid of everything that slows me down, especially sin that distracts me, because when I'm distracted, that's when this negative, destructive attitude comes up in my heart. I start to hear critical words – real or imagined, it doesn't matter. And I start meditating on those critical words instead of the Word of God. Meditating on those things shuts down the frontal lobe where I can process like an adult, and then I have no peace, no answers, and no understanding. I'm not operating from wisdom. I'm wondering why I'm acting like a twelve-year-old. It's because I'm functioning with a twelve-year-old's brain. After all, they don't have their frontal lobe developed yet. All these negative emotions shut down your ability to respond as an adult.

FEAR OR LOVE — EXPECTATIONS

The most influential authority figure in my life was an angry parent. I was afraid of doing anything wrong that would bring her punishment onto me. I was afraid of making a mistake. I was a child; I needed to learn how to do things, but I wasn't taught. Yet, my mother still had the expectation of me doing things the right way. She didn't teach me how to make a bed her way, but I remember the intense anger, yelling, and belittling I received for not tucking the sheets in correctly. It got to the point where I was afraid to do anything because I might get it wrong and feel her anger, so I decided to just sit on the couch as much as possible and stay out of her line of fire. It produced procrastination in me, and it caused me to do nothing rather than attempt something and endure the repercussions of her displeasure. I believed the lie that if I didn't do anything, I wouldn't be hurt and shamed. I lived my life expecting the other shoe to drop. The "app" running in the unconsciousness of my mind was fear-based, so even with all of the opportunities presented to me over my life, I was afraid to act. When I did act, I tended to make big mistakes as a result of a self-fulfilling, negative expectation. I expected to fail. So, I made an inner vow: I just won't do anything except what I want, when I want. That didn't quite work out for me!

Today, as I learn the language of the Covenant of Love with God, I know He is always good and ALL things work for the good of those who love Him. We are loved because God is love, and we are His beloved. He's not angry. He's not punishing. Religion punishes and is critical, but God disciplines and corrects us. He does it to protect us because He's a good Father, and that's what good fathers do. He loves us the way we are all the time, and He doesn't withhold His love for us if we don't get things perfect. He can't; that wouldn't be love. He is ravished by our most pathetic response. He's delighted by us.

Knowing that the God of Love is for me, I expect that all things work for me and not against me. My mistakes become messages of hope. I believe that goodness and mercy follow me. His love never fails, so I can trust Him and even learn to trust myself. I know what His love letters in the Bible are saying to me no matter what circumstances are around me. He is kind and compassionate. He is patient and merciful. I expect great things in my life because I serve a Great God and a Good King. I am learning to be loved, to trust, and to look forward with great anticipation for all of the days of my life!

I had a friend once say, "I didn't think it was a banner day when I woke up in Mexico in a warehouse full of marijuana with fifty Federales with guns pointed at me. I have learned not to judge if it's a good day or a bad day. That day ended up being the best day of my life. It was a wake-up call, and now I am really living."

I reframe days and events now with this mindset: These things aren't happening *to me*. They are happening *for me*. I don't *have* to do this. I *get* to do this.

Here is my daily decree:

"I expect today to be a great day! I serve the God of love, and all things work for my good. He never fails me."

I expect great doors of opportunity to open before me as I put my trust in Him! I don't live by sight, but I do live by faith. If today doesn't seem to be a good day, I will declare it to be again and again and again! He never fails. I will be able to look back and see where God has used my mistakes and given me the authority and power to overcome them.

REFLECTIONS:

- Do you ever catch yourself reacting to situations with an extremely intense emotional response?
- What are your daily expectations? Do you expect the other shoe to drop, or do you expect to be followed by goodness and mercy?

ACTION STEPS:

When your emotions get intense, pause and remove yourself from the situation. Ask God where the pain and intensity might be reminding you of something from your past.

Choose to forgive, release, and repent of judgments made against others and forgive them for their judgments against you.

Declare Godly expectations over your day every morning by looking at the psalms where David put his expectation and hope in God.

7

FOOD FOR THOUGHT

> *"May God himself, the God who makes everything holy and whole, make you holy and whole, put you together–spirit, soul, and body– and keep you fit for the coming of our Master, Jesus Christ. The One who called you is completely dependable. If he said it, he'll do it!"*
> 1 Thessalonians 5:23-24 (NIV)

My eating disorders started when I was in junior high when I bought a box of icing, ate the whole thing, and then threw it up. I had such shame over my body, even at that early age. I took dancing, ballet in particular, for about four hours a day, five or six days a week. I weighed ninety-five pounds. I was definitely not fat, but I saw myself as fat. I had a distorted view of myself. Anorexia and bulimia were not words that people knew back then. I actually saw a doctor to get some help because I didn't know what was going on, and he didn't know, either.

What I believe now is that a "sweet tooth" can be a generational curse passed down from generation to generation. My alcoholic grandmother used to hide her alcohol and her chocolates. We loved going over to Mimi's house because it was like a treasure hunt looking for candy.

When I got out of the mental institution in 2011 and was powerfully touched by the love of God, I felt Him tell me to quit eating sugar. I went through intense withdrawals. It was easier for me to quit cocaine and to quit smoking than it was for me to quit sugar. It was horrible. I remember buying watermelons in an effort to get a sugar fix to take the edge off the cravings. Fruit has a different type of sugar than the processed, refined sugar they put in almost everything we eat these days. Fun fact: they also put sugar in American cigarettes. Dr. Mark Hyman said on *CBS This Morning* that when they study animals, "they find that the rats go for the sugar and that it's eight times as addictive as cocaine. Small amounts of sugar can be part of a normal diet, but most of us are addicted to sugar and don't know it." Hyman himself has gone as far as calling sugar and sugary foods "deadly."

About two years ago, I went on a retreat with a group of women; everybody brought treats to share, like fudge or cookies. I wasn't in the habit of eating sugar anymore, but on day four, I thought, "Oh, come on. Just a little bit won't hurt." So I had a little bit. And then I thought, "Well, now that I'm off the wagon, I should enjoy it while I can. This will only be a few days, right?" I would continually dive into the fudge, which today I call sugar crack because it had the same effect on me.

The last day of the retreat, my friend Beth said something to me flippant and off the cuff, the way friends often do, and for some reason it hit me wrong. I came home from the retreat, and I couldn't stop thinking about it. "Why are some people so mean?" I thought. "I thought Beth and I were good friends. I can't believe she said that about me and thought it was funny." I was sad and hurt, and I began to wonder why I even had friends if it was going to be like that all the time. "I can't trust anyone," I thought. "You think you know someone, and then they do something like this." I moped around about it for two days, obsessing on the hurt and the pain and the feeling of betrayal. On day three, when my body had detoxed from sugar, thinking about that same incident didn't bother me at all. I realized that my feelings had been distorted by whatever the sugar did to my body, my brain, and my ability to process and regulate emotions.

Before I went into the alcohol treatment center, I was suffering from depression, and I knew that alcohol, which is full of sugar alcohols, was a depressant. I thought my depression was my biggest problem because I told myself I could quit drinking any time I wanted, and I just never wanted to. But when I did want to, I found that I couldn't quit drinking. I was ready to quit drinking, not because I really cared about how unmanageable my life was, but because I couldn't deal with the emotional pain.

My body's reaction to sugar in my food and sugar in alcohol was depression, and it distorted my ability to see and perceive things with any stability or balance. It distorted my perception of the reality going on around me. I've come to realize that sugar, flour, and processed foods are not my friends. Now I like to ingest non-GMO and whole foods, and one-ingredient foods like eggs, butter, milk, apples, or asparagus. I stay away from seed oils or vegetable oils because I've learned that those also have inflammatory effects similar to sugar.

Depression is inflammation of the brain. When I put down the sugar, my brain began to heal, and I was able to see things more clearly. I discovered things weren't nearly as catastrophic as I thought they were. In fact, when I detoxed from both alcohol and sugar, my life improved immensely. I challenge you to look at what you're eating, and then maybe look at what's eating you!

HUNGER

Did you know that whenever you pursue anything with a passion (hunger, crave, desire), it releases dopamine? We have heard the jokes about retail therapy. If I desire the new shoes, it will release dopamine. However, I will soon feel "down" and need to repeatedly shop to get my retail "fix." Every time I do that, I build up a tolerance, so I need more to get the same high.

If I desire the food intensely, it will release "feel good" chemicals in my body. Yet, if I get off-balance with food, I will need to eat more food to get the same release the next time, and the next time. We call it "comfort food" when it is high in fats and refined carbs. God created us to use food to heal our bodies, but I find when I get uncomfortable with my emotions (stress), I distract myself with "comfort food" instead of turning to the Comforter.

I remember my first time on a mission trip to Mozambique. There was no air-conditioning . . . at all. I am used to being in a climate-controlled environment, so if I get uncomfortable, I adjust the thermostat. I didn't have that option in Africa. It was hot ALL of the time. I drank tons of water every day and sweated it out! There was no relief day or night. I had not been so uncomfortable in my life! I found a young native kid who was selling giant candy bars outside of the base where I was staying, and I started buying giant candy bars two or three times a day. I had never bought king-size candy bars in America in all of my life, but I felt it was a necessity in Africa.

When I got back to America, a friend called me. Her husband had been at the same base at the same time that I was there. She remarked that her husband had dropped twelve pounds in about two weeks. She asked me how much weight I had lost. I weighed myself and discovered I had gained about five pounds! I was finding comfort in the comfort food instead of the Comforter.

TRUE LOVE

I remember "being in love," but the newness always wore off. Then I would find another "love." Was it real love, or a false fix that released feel-good hormones but had no stable foundation? As long as I was pursuing "false love" my way, my relationships were very temporary and transitional. Once the dopamine wore off, he wasn't making me happy anymore. However, I had become addicted to the drama, and it had become a habit. Pursuing false love is habit-forming.

It says in Matthew 5:6, *"Blessed are those who hunger and thirst after righteousness (right-mindedness, right wiseness), for they will be filled."* When I hunger and thirst for True Love instead of false love, there are no consequences. There are consequences to hungering and thirsting after those other things – like spending too much time and money shopping to feel better and breaking my budget, or medicating my emotions with comfort food and becoming unhealthy, or being ashamed of my lack of self-control, resulting in self-hate and self-destruction. The temporary "high" brings a painful "low."

Before I was set free, I was a slave to my habits. "I could quit anytime I wanted to," I said to myself and others. The truth was that I did want to quit smoking, overeating, overspending, pursuing dead-end relationships, etc., but I didn't know how or have the desire to learn. I hated the rules of the "establishment" because I thought they were restrictive.

I came to the end of myself. My best thinking – the ways I thought were going to let me live "free" and have "freedom" to do what makes me happy – brought me to the point where something radical had to happen or I was going to make a radical, permanent change by taking my own life. I called out to God in rage, fear, hate, and accusation against Him, yet I was also asking Him for help. I expected punishment, anger, and death to answer me because that's what I believed He was, but the God of Mercy and Compassion met me instead.

I didn't recognize the God of Christianity because I had been taught incorrectly about His nature and character. Yet, out of all the gods that I had learned of and followed, He was the One I cried out to when I had seconds before I pulled the trigger and chose to end my life. Now, I have learned and experienced the God of Love. I learned He is the One who is pursuing me because He is so in love with me. He is what I was always looking for in a bottle, a man, money, materialism, and in my own heart. He was the missing link to true freedom, and my life is living proof of that! As I learned who He is, I learned who I am. He's a good Father! He's not angry, disappointed, or ready to punish me; that was the reflection of my own heart and soul that needed and still desires more healing and freedom.

I read the Bible through a different lens today. My perceptions about God, myself, and others have changed. Now, I have a passion for life. I have a reason for being. Now, I have hope. I am continuing to hunger and thirst for more of Him, His ways, and His truth, and I receive more stability, love, joy, and peace as I do that.

REFLECTIONS:

- Do you ever turn to TV, food, shopping, sugar, wine, etc., instead of turning to God?
- Do you recognize garbage in, garbage out when it comes to what you've eaten and your mood the next day?
- Food was the first issue in the garden, and it was what Satan tempted Jesus with in the wilderness. Does food have addictive power over you?

ACTION STEPS:

Challenge yourself to commit to not eating any processed foods or processed oils (vegetable, seed oils) for thirty days and see how it affects your thinking. (Hint: if you can't identify the ingredients, it is processed.)

8

LOVE IS THE ANSWER

> *"You are always and dearly loved by God! So robe yourself with virtues of God, since you have been divinely chosen to be holy. Be merciful as you endeavor to understand others, and be compassionate, showing kindness toward all. Be gentle and humble, unoffendable in your patience with others. Tolerate the weaknesses of those in the family of faith, forgiving one another in the same way you have been graciously forgiven by Jesus Christ.*
> *If you find fault with someone, release this same gift of forgiveness to them. For love is supreme and must flow through each of these virtues. Love becomes the mark of true maturity."*
> Colossians 3:12-14 (TPT)

It seems as far back as I can possibly remember, I was being accused of something. I didn't know why the finger-pointing, criticizing, condemning, and shaming behavior towards me was going on, so in my child mind, I just believed there was something wrong with me. I even jumped in there in agreement with my mother and our generational attitude habits and constantly accused myself of things. Everything felt negative, critical, condemning, and judging. When I got older, if my life was hard, I convinced myself that I could point my finger at someone else as the cause. They were the reason why this was happening. It was obviously the reasonings of a wounded and traumatized soul. I've learned today that I am 100% responsible for the way my life goes.

DISCERNING OR ACCUSING?

When I was in the treatment center in my mid-thirties, I could not wait until family weekend came around and my parents would find out how they were responsible for the way I was. When they walked in, the counselor looked at them, and they hung their heads in shame. This was my validation! But then, the counselor told them they needed to cut me off, financially and every other way, if I wasn't willing to change. She told them I was suffering from a disease of gross immaturity and that I wanted to blame them and others for my adult decisions. The counselor said I needed to grow up or die.

I was shocked. I thought, "Wait a minute, this is not the way this is supposed to work out." But she was right. I had to grow up. I didn't have any adult skills. Bipolar drug addicts don't have skills. Basically, what the counselor told them was that I was not a victim. At this point in my life, I was a volunteer. I was responsible for my emotional health, relational health, spiritual health, physical health, and my nutritional health. As long as I was doing the finger-pointing, there were no solutions.

There is no hope in thinking of yourself as the victim. And there will be no hope for any change in our lives or our families as long as we do. We have a tendency as adults to point at people and not focus on the issues. We all must take responsibility for our part. Jesus did not die for us to be victims. We are victors. We need to no longer be drinking milk, but to be eating meat and grow up in Christ, because Colossians says that love is the mark of true maturity

(Hebrews 5:12-14, Colossians 3:14, TPT). Love believes the best. It sees the best. The critical, judging, condemning, and finger-pointing keeps us divided.

What if, instead of finger-pointing, criticizing, or condemning others for their behavior or flaws, we prayed for them instead? If we see flaws in others but not through the lens of love, it is not discernment. It is critical and judgmental. Could that be the antichrist spirit in the church keeping us blind?

IS IT HARMONY OR HOSTILITY?

One day when I was reading Romans 5:10, the word "hostile" jumped out at me: *"For if while we were **hostile** to God we were reconciled to Him through the death of His Son, it is still more certain that now that we are reconciled, we shall obtain salvation through Christ's life."* I looked it up in the dictionary. I also got a thesaurus out, and I made a list of synonyms and antonyms for *hostile*. The root of hostility is bitterness. The list of synonyms I made showed the fruit of hostility, but the root was bitterness.

Hostile means "of or pertaining to an enemy." If you are hostile, you have enmity or ill will toward someone or something. You are in opposition to that person or thing. The root word, *host*, is positive: taking care of a guest. But when you add *ile* (ill will), you are treating that guest as an enemy. Or as I like to think of it, you are hosting ill will. I only want to host the Holy Spirit! I do not want to "host" another, especially if it is coming from the root of bitterness.

Bitterness is unfulfilled revenge. Wherever we have bitterness, we have cold love and hardness of heart toward people and God. *"And then many will be offended, will betray one another, and will hate one another. Then many false prophets will rise up and deceive many. And because lawlessness will abound, the love of many will grow cold"* (Matthew 24:10, NKJV). We may not like what a person does or says, but we know that love never fails. We have no option but to love and pray for our enemies as Jesus taught us (Matthew 5:43-45). Opinions turn into negative attitudes, and negative attitudes turn into hard hearts. If we withdraw our love from people, we also withdraw from God without even realizing it. If we can't love a sister or a brother whom we can see, how can we love God whom we can't see (1 John 4:20)? None of us want to believe that we would ever turn our backs on God, but it happens every day when cold love is the result of offense.

At some point in our lives, we will all be hurt by someone, and intentionally or not, we will all cause a hurt *to* someone. We need to extend the same grace to others that we want to have extended to us. Jesus put it like this, *"Father, forgive them, for they know not what they do"* (Luke 23:34 AMPC). Jesus doesn't withdraw from us, because love never fails. We cannot withdraw from each other when we see weakness in others and call it love. It actually shows we have a lack of love.

LOVE IS THE ANTIDOTE

When I came back into the church – suicidal, addicted, and raging at everyone about everything – I frightened people. Although I was raised in the church and graduated from a Bible College, I was full of bitterness and judgments, and I was blind to all the love Jesus and others had for me. Yet there were some brave, loving, people who loved the torment and brokenness right out of me. They loved me when I was unlovable and undeserving of any kindness whatsoever. They are still in my life, loving me thirteen years later.

Love sees the best in everyone. Jesus died for everyone, and we are all created in His image and in His likeness. The antidote for bitterness, judgment, and offense is love. *"Love is patient. Love is kind. Love isn't jealous. It doesn't sing its own praises. It isn't arrogant. It isn't rude. It doesn't think about itself. It isn't irritable. It doesn't keep track of wrongs. It isn't happy when injustice is done, but it is happy with the truth. Love never stops being patient, never stops believing, never stops hoping, never gives up. Love never comes to an end"* (1Corinthians 13:4-8, GW).

The condition of our hearts has a profound effect on how we view God, ourselves, and others. Our judgments, our attitudes, and our unforgiveness cloud our view, making it distorted like that fun house mirror. The enemy wants to keep our perception distorted so we can't love God, ourselves, or others like we should. Love is something that requires action and exercise, like a muscle, to stay strong. We must grow in love, or we will become lukewarm – or even cold – and walk away from God. The pathway of turning away from God can start with just one offense or one judgement, and we can't assume it won't happen to us. It happened to me, and I lived with absolute pain and torment for over thirty years because of my twisted perceptions of God, myself, and others. It is just by the grace and mercy of God I am alive today.

I have prayers for you in the following pages. I encourage you to sit with God and ask Him where you may have some housecleaning to do in your temple. I pray that you have a different perspective toward God, yourself, and others after reading this book, and that you see everything differently as a result. You are loved. Be blessed. God is so good!

Just remember:

It's not because we are good, but because He is good.

It's not because we are worthy, but because He is worthy.

It's not because we deserve it, but because He deserves the reward of His suffering.

All we have to do is confess, forgive, repent, and renounce. He did the hard part on the cross for us.

REFLECTIONS:

- In what areas can you grow in love, especially towards the unlovable?
- Instead of judging and withdrawing, where could you be humble and help others grow and heal by honoring and loving well?

ACTION STEPS:

Speak these declarations daily:

I don't judge, and I'm not judged.

I don't condemn, and I'm not condemned.

I don't criticize, and I'm not criticized.

The love of God is shed abroad in my heart by the power of the Holy Spirit.

God opposes the proud but gives grace to the humble.

I speak truth in love (Eph 4:15, NIV). Those who promote peace have joy (Proverbs 12:20, NIV).

ACKNOWLEDGMENTS

I am first of all grateful for my mother and father, Ray & Una Mae Eldridge, for introducing me to Jesus Christ, which is the most beautiful and important thing that could ever be done for a child. They stood by me and encouraged me in my walk with Him, and I am forever grateful.

I am also grateful to the following people who have contributed to me even being alive today. Many of them were with me in the beginning and are still standing with me today. They carry mature love, and they love well. They loved the unloveable, and that was definitely me when I first came to Christ. I was and still am loved even when I didn't deserve love. That is the mark of Christ. I would like to thank:

Pastors Doug & Rosemary Lowery - Maranatha Assembly of God, Decatur, IL; Pastors Happy & Dianne Leman - The Vineyard Church, Urbana, IL; Jack & Lynn Greenwood - Resurrection Life Church, Decatur, IL; Larry Duncan - Director of The Guiding Light Healing Room; Mary Turek; Anita Mason - therapist and Director of Joshua Company Ministries; Sonya Evans; Timothy Fote; Nora Moragas; Brenda Reynolds; Katie Simmons; Walt & Carol Pilcher; George & Pat Nizynski; Chester & Betsy Kylstra - Restoring The Foundations Ministry Founders; Dr Edna Riley - Mentor & RTF Trainer/Board Member; Phyllis & Denny Schemenske -

RTF Trainers; Nancy Economou - Watts of Love; Dr. Norm & Angel Poorman - United Resource Alliance; Jo & Dan Caulkins; Emelyn Hart; Dr Randy Clark - Global Awakening; Will & Musy Hart - Iris Global; Dr Heidi Baker - co-founder of Iris Global; Dr Rodney Hogue; Larry and Laura Randolph - Peytonsville Baptist Church, Thompson's Station, TN; Barbara Ann Jeter - Eternal Heiress Ministries; Missy Maxwell Worton - Warrior Writers; and Ashley Hagan - my amazingly patient editor at Inkwell Writers Publishing Services.

ABOUT LYNN ELDRIDGE

Lynn Eldridge was raised in the church, but at fifteen, bipolar disorder, eating disorders, and addictions began to take over her life. After thirty-five years of a life of devastation, she felt like life wasn't worth living and contemplated suicide. Friends prayed for her life, and soon after her release from a mental institution, she had a powerful encounter with God and was set free!

Lynn is now an itinerate speaker and is the author of *Bipolar To Beloved* with its companion workbook (#1 Amazon New Release) where she shares her story of recovery. She is ordained with Global Awakening and is a conference leader for Restoring the Foundations inner healing and deliverance ministry. You can contact Lynn for speaking engagements at contact@lynneldridge.com.

Other Books by Lynn Eldridge

Scan to find out more!

ABOUT DR. RANDY CLARK

Dr. Randy Clark is a noted international speaker and best-selling author of multiple books, including *There is More*. He is best known for being used of God to birth the revival in Toronto, Canada, in 1994 that continued six nights a week for twelve years. Out of that he birthed Global Awakening, a global community of believers empowered to awaken the world. Learn more at globalawakening.com.

If you liked this book, you might enjoy the following:

Dr Randy Clark
Authority To Heal
There Is More! The Secret To Experiencing God's Power To Change Your Life
The Biblical Guidebook To Deliverance
The Essential Guide To Healing
Intimacy with God: Cultivating a Life of Deep Friendship Through Obedience

Tyler Fellar
Don't Stop: 365 Daily Devotions to Ignite Your Purpose

Will Hart
Godrunner: Your Place in God's Big Story

Dr. Rodney Hogue
Forgiveness
Liberated: Set Free and Staying Free from Demonic Strongholds

Dr. Mike Hutchings
Supernatural Breakthrough From The Captivity of Trauma

Larry Randolph
Spirit Talk: Hearing the Voice of God
User Friendly Prophecy
Original Breath
Finding Your Sphere of Influence
Up & Down (audio CD)

APPENDIX

PRAYERS AND DECLARATIONS

Below are some scriptures to personalize, declare, and meditate on daily:

> *"Don't pick on people, jump on their failures, criticize their faults–unless, of course, you want the same treatment. Don't condemn those who are down; that hardness can boomerang. Be easy on people; you'll find life a lot easier. Give away your life; you'll find life given back, but not merely given back–given back with bonus and blessing. Giving, not getting, is the way. Generosity begets generosity."*
> Luke 6:37-38 (MSG)

> *"Make sure that everyone has kindness from God so that bitterness doesn't take root and grow up to cause trouble that corrupts many of you."*
> Hebrews 12:15 (GW)

"Honor (esteem and value as precious) your father and your mother-this is the first commandment with a promise-[Exodus 20:12.] That all may be well with you and that you may live long on the earth."
Ephesians 6:2-3 (AMPC)

"Do not judge, or you too will be judged. For in the same way you judge others, you will be judged, and with the measure you use, it will be measured to you."
Matthew 7:1-2 (NIV)

"Carry each other's burdens, and in this way you will fulfill the law of Christ."
Galatians 6:2 (NIV)

"No matter who you are, if you judge anyone, you have no excuse. When you judge another person, you condemn yourself, since you, the judge, do the same things. When you judge people for doing these things but then do them yourself, do you think you will escape God's judgment?"
Romans 2:1, 3 (GW)

PRAYER FOR BITTER ROOT JUDGMENTS

Father, in the name of Jesus, I confess my sin of judging _____ for _____ and for any negative emotions, thoughts, and attitudes against me (example: she's selfish, uncaring, prideful, etc.)_____.

I ask you to forgive me for judging, criticizing, and accusing _____ and for partnering with the powers of darkness. I renounce and break agreement with the kingdom of darkness I made over _____'s life.

I choose to forgive and bless _____.

I also choose to forgive myself.

I ask you, Lord, to break the sowing and reaping cycle I set up with the bitter judgments over my life. I ask you, Holy Spirit, to breathe on the seeds I sowed of bitterness and break their power with the power of the blood of Jesus Christ. I pray the fullness of your blessing and your will in _____'s life and in my own.

In Jesus' name.

PRAYER FOR DISHONORING PARENTS

I especially ask forgiveness, Lord, for dishonoring my _____(mother or father) by judging them for _____(example: the way they handled their finances, relationships, etc.). I ask you, God, to forgive me for judging and dishonoring them and for how I may have judged and dishonored You. I also choose to forgive myself. I renounce and break that sowing and reaping cycle that I set up with the kingdom of darkness in the name of Jesus Christ.

PRAYER FOR BITTER ROOT EXPECTATIONS

Forgive me for expecting the kingdom of darkness to go before me instead of the God of Angel Armies to go before me. I renounce the self-fulfilling prophecies I made with the kingdom of darkness.

I declare and establish the kingdom of Heaven as I go.

I declare God's will on earth as it is in heaven. I take authority over every regional, territorial, generational, and familiar spirit. I forbid it to manifest against me or through me. I declare the atmosphere where I go today will be filled with love, joy, and peace.

SYNONYMS AND ANTONYMS

"Fill your thoughts with my words until they penetrate deep into your spirit. Then, as you unwrap (define these words - my understanding) my words, they will impart true life and radiant health into the very core of your being."
Proverbs 4:21-22 (TPT)

Loved	Hated	**Kind,**	Rude, Critical
Pure	Hostile	**Cheerful, Satisfied**	Surly, Judgmental
Gracious	Disvalue, Cold	**Good-tempered**	Crusty, Condemning
Considerate	Abrupt,	**Calm,**	Unkind
Attentive	Blunt,	**Humble**	Selfish
Polite	Brusque, Insulting	**Likeable, Meek**	Mean
Thoughtful	Curt,	**Attentive**	Self-centered
Courteous	Gruff	**Compassion**	Malicious
Agreeable	Sharp, Bitter	**Tender**	Insensitive
Friendly	Snippy,	**Merciful**	Harsh
Considerate	Discourteous	**Soft,**	Severe
Agreeable	Disagreeable	**Patient**	Stern
Well-mannered	Ill-mannered	**Selfless**	Cruel, Vicious,
Gentle, Appreciative, Grateful	Impolite, Blunt		

DIS- WORDS

DIS: Ruler of the Roman underworld

Disability	Disfigured	Disquiet
Disagreeable	Disfunction (dys)	Disregard
Disappear	Dishonest	Disrespect
Disappointed	Dishonor	Disrobe
Disapprove	Disingenuous	Dissatisfied
Discombobulate	Disintegration	Dissent
Disconnected	Disjoint	Dissipate
Discontent	Disliked	Dissolution
Discontinue	Dislocate	Dissolve
Discord	Dismissed	Distance
Discourage	Disobedience	Distemper
Discourse	Disoriented	Distract
Discourteous	Disown	Distraught
Discredit	Displace	Distressed
Disdain	Displeasure	Distrust
Disengage	Disqualify	Disturbed

RE- WORDS

RE - back or again

React	Redeem	Rekindle	Resist
Realignment	Redefine	Release	Resolution
Reboot	Rediscover	Relocate	Resonate
Rebound	Reestablish	Remain	Resource
Recalibrate	Reference	Remarry	Response
Receptical	Refine	Remember	Rest
Recharge	Reflect	Remind	Restoration
Reclaim	Reform	Renew	Resuscitate
Recognize	Refresh	Repaid	Retort
Recommend	Regard	Repair	Return
Recompense	Regenerate	Repent	Reverse
Reconcile	Reignite	Replace	Revise
Reconnect	Reinstate	Replenish	Revisit
Recording	Rejoice	Reply	Revitalize
Recovery	Rejoin	Reset	Revive
Recreate	Rejuvenate	Resilient	Rewind

MORE SCRIPTURES ABOUT ATTITUDES

"Those who live by the corrupt nature have the corrupt nature's attitude. But those who live by the spiritual nature have the spiritual nature's attitude. The corrupt nature's attitude leads to death. But the spiritual nature's attitude leads to life and peace. This is so because the corrupt nature has a hostile attitude toward God. It refuses to place itself under the authority of God's standards because it can't."
Romans 8:5-7 (GW)

"Do not merely listen to the word, and so deceive yourselves. Do what it says. Anyone who listens to the word but does not do what it says is like someone who looks at his face in a mirror and, after looking at himself, goes away and immediately forgets what he looks like. But whoever looks intently into the perfect law that gives freedom, and continues in it–not forgetting what they have heard, but doing it–they will be blessed in what they do."
James 1:22-25 (NIV)

"And although you at one time were estranged and alienated from Him and were of hostile attitude of mind in your wicked activities."
Colossians 1:21 (AMPC)

"He must not be a new convert, or he may [develop a beclouded and stupid state of mind] as the result of pride [be blinded by conceit, and] fall into the condemnation that the devil [once] did. [Isa. 14:12-14.]"
1 Timothy 3:6, AMPC

"The precepts of the Lord are right, rejoicing the heart; the commandment of the Lord is pure and bright, enlightening the eyes."
Psalm 19:8 (AMPC)

"Jesus answered, 'Nicodemus, listen to this eternal truth: Before a person can even perceive God's kingdom, they must first experience a rebirth.'"
John 3:3 (TPT)

"Children, obey your parents [as God's representatives] in all things, for this [attitude of respect and obedience] is well-pleasing to the Lord [and will bring you God's promised blessings]."
Colossians 3:20 (AMPC)

"That's why I teach the people using parables, because they think they're looking for truth, yet because their hearts are unteachable, they never discover it. Although they will listen to me, they never fully perceive the message I speak."
Matthew 13:13 (TPT)

"Jesus turned to Peter and said, 'Get out of my way, you Satan! You are a hindrance to me, because your thoughts are only filled with man's VIEWPOINTS and not with the ways of God.'"
Matthew 16:23 (TPT)

"The prophecy of Isaiah describes them perfectly: Although they listen carefully to everything I speak, they don't understand a thing I say. They look and pretend to see, but the eyes of their hearts are closed. Their minds are dull and slow to perceive, their ears are plugged and are hard of hearing, and they have deliberately shut

their eyes to the truth. Otherwise they would open their eyes to see, and open their ears to hear, and open their minds to understand. Then they would turn to me and I would instantly heal them."
Matthew 13:14-15 (TPT)

"Forgive my failures as a young man, and overlook the sins of my immaturity. Give me grace, Yahweh! Always look at me through your eyes of love– your forgiving eyes of mercy and compassion. When you think of me, see me as one you love and care for."
Psalms 25:6-7 (TPT)

"Since each of you are part of God's family never complain or grumble about each other so that judgment will not come on you, for the true Judge is near and very ready to appear!"
James (Jacob) 5:9 (TPT)

"However, you were taught to have a new attitude."
Ephesians 4:23 (GW)

"If you have a willing attitude and obey, then you will again eat the good crops of the land."
Isaiah 1:19 (NET)

"So let each individual first evaluate his own attitude and only then eat the bread and drink the cup."
1 Corinthians 11:28 (TPT)

"The attitude that comes from selfishness leads to death, but the attitude that comes from the Spirit leads to life and peace. So the attitude that comes from selfishness is hostile to God. It doesn't submit to God's Law, because it can't. People who are self-centered aren't able to please God."
Romans 8:6-8 (CEB)

"We can demolish every deceptive fantasy that opposes God and break through every arrogant ATTITUDE that is raised up in defiance of the true knowledge of God. We capture, like prisoners of war, every thought and insist that it bow in obedience to the Anointed One."
2 Corinthians 10:5 (TPT)

A scoffer seeks Wisdom in vain [for his very attitude blinds and deafens him to it], but knowledge is easy to him who [being teachable] understands.
Proverbs 14:6 (AMPC)

Their attitude blinds them "For the word of God is alive and active. Sharper than any double-edged sword, it penetrates even to dividing soul and spirit, joints and marrow; it judges the thoughts and attitudes of the heart."
Hebrews 4:12 (NIV)

"Do not harden your hearts, as [happened] in the rebellion [of Israel] and their provocation and embitterment [of Me] in the day of testing in the wilderness."
Hebrews 3:8 (AMPC)

"Then while it is [still] called Today, if you would hear His voice and when you hear it, do not harden your hearts as in the rebellion [in the desert, when the people provoked and irritated and embittered God against them]. [Ps. 95:7, 8.]"
Hebrews 3:15 (AMPC)

"You were taught, with regard to your former way of life, to put off your old self, which is being corrupted by its deceitful desires; to be made new in the ATTITUDE of your minds; and to put on the new self, created to be like God in true righteousness and holiness."
Ephesians 4:22-24 (NIV)

"By this we come to know (progressively to recognize, to perceive, to understand) the [essential] love: that He laid down His [own] life for us; and we ought to lay [our] lives down for [those who are our] brothers [in Him]."
1 John 3:16 (AMPC)

"I looked [them over] and rose up and said to the nobles and officials and the other people, Do not be afraid of the enemy; [earnestly] remember the Lord and IMPRINT Him [on your minds], great and terrible, and [take from Him courage to] fight for your brethren, your sons, your daughters, your wives, and your homes."
Nehemiah 4:14 (AMPC)

"I will remember the deeds of the Lord. I will remember your ancient miracles. I will reflect on all your actions and think about what you have done."
Psalms 77:11-12 (GW)

"Everything seems to go wrong when you FEEL weak and depressed. But when you choose to be cheerful, every day will bring you more and more joy and fullness."
Proverbs 15:15 (TPT)

www.ingramcontent.com/pod-product-compliance
Lightning Source LLC
Chambersburg PA
CBHW052147070526
44585CB00017B/2019